❧ From Acre End ❧

FROM ACRE END
Portrait of a Village

MOLLIE HARRIS

To Chris,
Happy Easter and
Good Luck in your
New Job.
With love from
Katie
. xxx.

Chatto & Windus · London

Published in paperback in 1986 by
Chatto & Windus Ltd
40 William IV Street
London WC2N 4DF

From Acre End was first published in Great Britain
by Chatto & Windus Ltd 1982

British Library Cataloguing in Publication Data
Harris, Mollie
From Acre End.
1. Eynsham (Oxfordshire) —— Social life and customs
I. Title
942.5'71   DA690.E98

ISBN 0-7011-3079-2

Printed and bound in Great Britain by
Butler & Tanner Ltd, Frome and London

❧ Contents ☙

List of Illustrations
Acknowledgements
Foreword *by Phil Drabble*
Introduction   11
Annette Faulkner   22
Alice May Batts   7
Margery Blake   33
Ernest William Ovenall   39
Ida Millicent Green   50
Ernest Edward Harris   54
Alice May Hilsdon   59
Albert Edward Ovenall   65
Dorothy Aldridge   68
Roy Blake   75
Ivy Hanks   80
Temperance Beatrice Hawtin   82
Winifred May Ellis and Ida Jane Hepenstall   87
Ida Mabel Anne Hopkins   90
Elsie May Green   93
Daisy Pratley   100
Hilda May Cooling   102
Harold A. Quainton   106
Jim Evans   111
Emily Bolton   121
William Thomas Grant   130
Charles Frederick Belcher   140
Leslie George Harris   142

Epilogue   151
The Eynsham Poaching Song   153

⊷ LIST OF ILLUSTRATIONS ⊶

1 Eynsham Morris group, 1937
   page 17
2 Acre End Street, 1906 *18*
3 Acre End Street, 1910 *18*
4 The Red Lion Inn, 1910 *19*
5 Newland Street, 1900 *19*
6 Eynsham High Street, early
   1920s *20*
7 Church Street *20*
8 Local advertising, 1905 *21*
9 Mrs Blake in pony and trap *26*
10 Alice May Clack, aged twenty-
   two *29*
11 The two young Miss Deanes *35*
12 Corn drilling with two horses *37*
13 One of the first steam ploughs *37*
14 The Board School, 1907 *41*
15 Mr Trethewy the headmaster *41*
16 Ernest Ovenall's school medals *41*
17 The Christmas postcard, 1910 *45*
18 The staff of the post office *46*
19 Ernest Ovenall in army uniform *49*
20 The Biggers family *51*
21 John Biggers with delivery van *53*
22 Children at the Infants' School *62*
23 Girls from the Board School,
   1912 *62*
24 A play at the Infants' School *63*
25 Sunday School treat at the
   Litchfield *63*
26 Class One at Eynsham School,
   1929 *64*
27 Girls from the Board School *64*
28 The Aldridge family at the Railway
   Inn *69*
29 Dorothy Aldridge's mother *74*
30 Bottles from Blake's lemonade
   factory *76*
31 Crochet-work pelmet *76*
32 The Railway Inn, 1907 *79*
33 The site of Blake's 'pop' factory *81*
34 Newland Street *89*

35 The bridge by the Talbot Inn *92*
36 Mr Floyd in 1880 *97*
37 John Floyd at the toll-gate, 1900 *97*
38 The Swinford toll bridge *98*
39 The toll bridge in the early 1900s *98*
40 The board from the toll-gate *99*
41 The Square *101*
42 One of the first of the bakers'
   vans *103*
43 Hilda Stevens and Baker Dore
   stacking bread *104*
44 Hilda Stevens and her mother *104*
45 A scene from Eynsham fair *105*
46 Cutting grass *114*
47 Cutting and baling hay *114*
48 An early reaping machine in
   use *118*
49 Jim Evans in the Field Artillery *118*
50 Jim Evans in chauffeur's
   uniform *120*
51 Pimm's shop *122*
52 A later photograph of Pimm's
   shop *122*
53 Children at the Infants' School,
   1912 *125*
54 Teachers at the Infants' School,
   1912 *126*
55 Group including Mrs 'Duke'
   Buckingham *127*
56 Eynsham railway station *133*
57 Outside the Hythe Croft, 1912 *137*
58 Mr Trethewy and local football
   team *137*
59 The Ovenall family, 1907 *138*
60 The Mumford family *138*
61 Three Mumford girls *139*
62 The Harris family *143*
63 Mrs 'Hog Pudding' Harris *143*
64 The sisters of 'Tailor' Harris *145*
65 A sister of 'Tailor' Harris *146*
66 'Tailor' Harris as a young man *146*
67 The Harris children *149*

❧ ACKNOWLEDGEMENTS ❧

Miss D. Aldridge, Mrs A. Batts, Mr F. Belcher, Mrs M. Blake, Mr R. Blake, Mrs E. Bolton, Mrs H. Cooling, Mrs W. Ellis, Mr J. Evans, Mrs A. Faulkner, Mr W. Grant, Mrs I. Green, Mrs E. Green, Mr E. Harris, Mr L. Harris, Mrs T. Hawtin, Mrs I. Hanks, Mrs A. Hilsdon, Mrs I. Hepenstall, Miss I. Hopkins, Mr A. Ovenall, Mr E. Ovenall, Mrs D. Pratley, Mr H. Quainton.

To all my friends and to many others who I have not named, I offer my most grateful thanks for their stories and photographs and information. In particular, I would like to thank Jim Evans for making his collection of photographs available. I have made every effort to ensure that the facts are accurate, having checked and rechecked again and again with those kind people who have readily given them to me. This is *their* story how they told it to me. Since going to print unfortunately a few of my old friends have passed away, but in every case I had their permission to go ahead with their story.

I would like to thank the following for permission to reproduce illustrations in which they own the copyright: the Westgate Library, Oxford (2, 3, 4, 5, 34); Packer's Studio, Chipping Norton (6, 7); Sue Chapman (30, 31, 33); Oxford and County Newspapers Ltd (38, 39, 51, 52); The Oxfordshire County Museum, Woodstock (40).

⋙ FOREWORD ⋘
PHIL DRABBLE

A symptom of our prepacked, disposable society is an overwhelming nostalgia for the 'good old days', when life was so much simpler and more predictable. The pressures of our modern rat race, where nobody is certain what tomorrow will bring – or even if there will be a tomorrow – make the more leisurely pace enjoyed by our ancestors seem as attractive as a perpetual holiday.

A casual dip into *From Acre End* will dispel such illusions. Children of twelve took the 'labour' exam which meant, if they passed it, that they were old enough – and qualified! – to leave school and begin their labours, which would continue for the rest of their lives.

Girls went into service before they were thirteen and might not return home, even for a holiday, for the next four or five years. Their wages were about four or five shillings a *month* – 20 or 25p in the washers that masquerade as currency in our progressive times. Grown men worked for a wage of £1 to £1. 5. 0. a week; and if they were ill they had to pay the doctor for his services.

But first impressions are traditionally misleading. This is a happy book, about delightful people, who enjoyed the simple things of life to the full instead of being dissatisfied with East Street, as is the fashion today.

From Acre End is really a history of the village of Eynsham told, as all history should be told, by word of mouth by the folk who have lived there for generations and grown up with the deep love that only solid roots can sustain.

Mollie Harris, the author, has been a friend of mine for more than thirty years, so I can vouch for the fact that she is no armchair historian, no dewy-eyed do-gooder but a practical countrywoman to the core. When I first knew her, she was as weatherbeaten as a gypsy from long hours in the fields, harvesting potatoes or hoeing turnips or gathering fruit or doing any of the other jobs on farms that are the traditional province of the 'casual' labourer.

Mollie's home-made jams and preserves make the 'convenience' mush from supermarkets seem rubbish by comparison, while the quality of her home-made wines would improve the standard of the most lavish expense-account meal.

She is a genuine countrywoman, deeply in love with her village so that, when she talks to her neighbours, they recount their family histories with a completely unselfconscious frankness.

The result is a true folk tale of the inhabitants and their lives at first hand, as history was handed down orally from generation to generation before the trendy sociologists of modern times warped it with their incessant whining about the discomfort of our feather-bedded society.

Mollie's friends and their ancestors shine through as *real* countryfolk who lived happy lives which made up for shortage of cash by enjoying creative work, with simple pleasures, spiced with humour and the capacity to appreciate the best in village life.

Mollie Harris and her friends have produced a record of life in the country that paints the picture, warts and all – and still leaves their readers with the firm conviction that their first impression of 'good old days' was no illusion after all!

PHIL DRABBLE

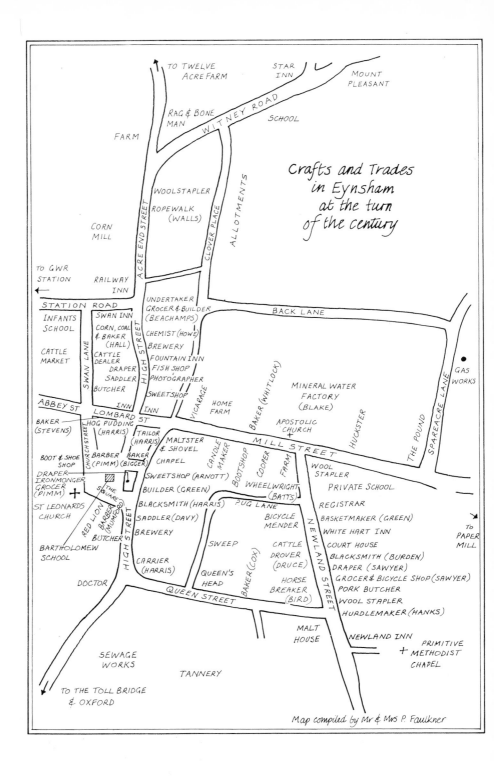

Crafts and Trades in Eynsham at the turn of the century

Map compiled by Mr & Mrs P. Faulkner

⇥ INTRODUCTION ⇤

This book is about the village of Eynsham in Oxfordshire, and the people who lived there in the first quarter of this century. I have called it *From Acre End* after one of the street names, and because, when I first came to live here over thirty years ago, one of the elderly men I used to talk to about the old days always referred to the village as Acre End, and said that when he was a lad a good many people called it that.

Eynsham lies in a lush green valley set between the rivers Thames and Evenlode. The Cotswolds begin to rise very gradually just west of the village, sheltering it from much of the cold, severe weather in winter. Oxford, with its dreaming spires and its giant car factories, lies a few miles to the east, and Witney, the famous blanket town, five miles to the west.

Eynsham was a large and go-ahead village even at the turn of the century – in those days it had its own privately owned gasworks, and main drainage and its own water supply was installed in 1903, at a time when many other towns and villages still had vault or bucket lavatories and water drawn from wells. But although it is handsome and pleasant enough – certainly to those of us who live there! – it is far from being a uniquely beautiful village of the kind one finds in the Cotswolds, nor is it celebrated for its historical or literary associations. It remains, as it was in the first quarter of this century, a very typical English working village: and because the lives of its late-Victorian and Edwardian inhabitants were so representative of those led by countless numbers of countryfolk at the time, I felt that these first-hand accounts would be of particular interest. By recreating my local community as it then was, I hoped to evoke and describe a way of life which, for good and ill, vanished for ever during the lives of those who remembered it for me.

Although Ancient Briton, Roman and Saxon remains have been found in the country around, Eynsham achieved a more than local fame in the Middle Ages. Its Benedictine Abbey was founded in 1005 and rebuilt after the Norman Conquest, between 1091 and 1109. The first abbot, Aelfric, spent many of his later years translating Bible stories into English for 'little boys of tender years so that they may be able to receive languages into their tender minds while they progressed to higher studies'; he also wrote one of the earliest English grammars, and was nicknamed 'Grammaticus'. The Abbey surrendered to Henry VIII in December 1539. The ruins stood until the seventeenth century, when they were used as a quarry: very little now remains, though carved pieces of stone from the Abbey can be seen built into cottages and garden walls.

At the turn of the century Eynsham retained – as it still retains – its mediaeval street plan, and looked much as it does now. Clustering round the Square and alongside the mediaeval parish church of St Leonard's stood several Cotswold stone cottages, with roofs of thatch or locally quarried Stonesfield slates. Much of the old part of the village was like this; gentry and business folk lived in the larger eighteenth- and nineteenth-century houses. Most cottages had long gardens at the back, filled with vegetables; at the end of each plot stood the familiar bucket or vault lavatory and a pig sty, both kept well out of the way, and for the same reason. Some cottagers kept a few hens; as well as providing the family with fresh eggs, the hens made a good meal when they got past laying. Like the pigs, they were fed all the scraps and old vegetables. Every day housewives would boil up an old saucepan of tiny 'pig taters' to help fatten the pigs, which were usually slaughtered in the back garden in the autumn, providing the family with plenty of fat bacon for the winter. For a few shillings a year, most people rented an allotment, which supplied plenty of vegetables for their large families. Boughten vegetables were unheard of, at least for the poor folk.

The chief occupation for the men was farming. At least ten farmers em-ployed a number of local men. With its high lime content, the soil was suitable for most crops: barley grew especially well, as did wheat, clover and sugar beet. The lush meadow land provided good grazing for cattle, while sheep did well on the higher gravelly ground. Much of the grassland was grown for hay, and several men were employed as hay-tiers and were kept busy baling and despatching by rail thousands of bales of hay and straw to London and the Midlands. Local folk also used the railway a certain amount, travelling usually to Oxford or Witney to shop or visit friends (Eynsham station was on the G.W.R. line between Oxford and Fairford, which was eventually closed in June 1962 to passenger traffic, but kept open for freight until 1970). And the carrier's cart still made the journey into Oxford on Mondays, Wednesdays (market day) and Saturdays, and to Witney on (hurdle) Thursdays, also a market day. At one time Eynsham itself held a market on Wednesdays, selling pigs, cattle and sheep: it was discontinued at some stage, probably at the outbreak of the First World War.

The population in 1901 was 1,757. By 1911 it had dropped slightly, most probably because of the closure of the local paper mill. Throughout the Middle Ages there was a flour mill in Eynsham, which belonged to the Abbey. The rent, payable yearly to the Abbot by the miller, was ten shillings and 450 eels: the eels were no doubt caught in the mill pond, and helped to feed the monks. After the dissolution of the monasteries, the mill passed into private hands, and was in use until 1650. At some stage during the next twenty years the mill became a paper mill, supplying white paper for the Bible presses. A certain George Hagar was granted a patent for 'an improved method of making white paper by sizing the pulp to the mortar', and it was here that the first experiments in making paper from esparto grass were carried out. But towards the end of the nineteenth century huge supplies of imported paper began to flood into the country: although the mill at Wolvercote thrived, and continues to make paper for the Bible presses, the one at Eynsham was closed down. Experienced men who had been employed there had to go further afield to look for similar work. For a while artificial leather made from off-cuts of cartridge cases was manufactured at the mill. The compressed cardboard was brought to Eynsham in wagon loads, and the finished 'leather' was eventually used to sole cheap boots and shoes. Not surprisingly, these tended to disintegrate when the wearer got them wet.

Later on the mill was used as a glue, rag and flock mill, and about fifty villagers worked there on day and night shifts. Rags were turned into cheap flock mattresses, of the kind that were then very popular, but the main manufacture was glue. By-products of the mill included bonemeal for fertilisers and bone powder for the manufacture of bone china. Great waggon loads of bones used to arrive by rail at Eynsham station. They were then hauled to the mill in carts, and people can still remember the smell of the bones, and the maggots that fell off the carts as they rumbled through the village and down the Hanborough Road. All this came to an end in the late 1920s: the buildings were demolished, and much of the rubble was used as ballast when the nearby A.40 was built in 1935. Today a trout farm thrives where the old mill once stood.

Also employing local folk were two breweries, a lemonade factory, three or four bakers, two butchers, the blacksmith and several grocers' shops. The two main grocers were Pimm's in the Square, and Sawyer's in Newland Street. Both these also sold hardware and ironmongery, but Sawyer's also dealt in gardening tools, boots and bikes, paints and paper, paraffin and pick-axes. There were several 'one man' and sometimes 'one woman' little businesses going on in the cottages. There was a hurdle-maker and a basket-maker, as well as housewives making sweets, rag balls and hog puddings – anything to earn a few pence. The village even had its own photographer, as well as a cattle-dealer, corn and coal merchants, wool staplers, a bicycle mender and a cattle drover. The village had an excellent practising chemist, who also doubled up as the sub-postmaster, employing four or five postmen, two boys and two telegraph ladies. There were two churches and two chapels: the Revd Nash Bricknell looked after the souls of the villagers, while Dr Cruickshank cared for their medical needs. There were at least a dozen pubs, two of which have since closed.

Many Eynsham men joined the forces during the First World War, and fifty-one of them lost their lives. Of those who returned, some turned their backs on the land and looked for easier work with better pay. In 1930 a new factory for processing sugar beet into sugar was opened, and seemed to offer great opportunities for the villagers, who were beginning to feel the effects of the Depression: but the factory closed after only a short time.

One small fly in the ointment was the toll gate a mile out of the village. Eynsham people have always resented having to pay to cross the bridge that spans the Thames here – and before the building of the A.40, this was the main route and the shortest route into Oxford. The bridge, which has survived virtually unchanged for over two hundred years, was built for the fourth Earl of Abingdon by authority of an Act of Parliament, and first opened to traffic in August 1769: it was built on the understanding that all money collected would be free of tax. At one time cyclists had to pay to cross, a halfpenny each way. Years ago three men from the village worked at the Chawley brick works in Cumnor, which were also owned by the Earl of Abingdon. A penny a day was a lot to come out of their wages, so one of them, a Mr Douglas, asked his foreman if he could speak to the Earl about it. An appointment was made and Mr Douglas, cap in hand, with the foreman standing by, said to the Earl, 'Your Lordship, there are three of us who work for you and each day we have to pay a halfpenny each time we come through your toll gate. Is there anything you can do to help us, Sir?' Without looking at Mr Douglas, the Earl asked his foreman to 'See that these men get an extra sixpence in their wages' – exactly what it cost them every week to cross the bridge.

In those days cattle being driven to Oxford market and sheep on their way to the big sheep sales were also charged to cross the bridge. Farmers had to pay a halfpenny a head for every bull, cow, steer, heifer and ox, and a farthing a head for sheep, lambs, calves and swine. One local farmer who always sold his sheep at Oxford market used to get the sheepdogs to 'run' the sheep just before they got to the toll gate, so that by the time they passed through the animals were going at such a pace that the tollkeeper was unable to count them. When he asked the farmer how many had passed through, the farmer would cunningly tell him two or three dozen fewer.

Eynsham was considered a very 'rough place' in the old days. Inhabitants can still remember the time when men who had no money to go to the pub would congregate outside one of them. A strong rough fellow would then take off his jacket and dangle and shake it in front of one of the pub windows in the hope that a fighting, drinking man inside would see and get the message – for the shaking of the jacket was a challenge to come out and fight its owner. It was also a friendly and close-knit community, in which nick-names were widely used: with perhaps five or six families all sharing the same surname, nicknames for each separate family was a must. Most people then attended church or chapel regularly, and the chapel Sunday School boasted an attendance of over one hundred children. There was a Young Man's social club, held at The Railway Inn – and a very vigorous group of Morris dancers, most of whom were farm labourers.

The villagers were – and still are – proud of their morris dancers. There has been a side for over 125 years in Eynsham, known as the Eynsham Morris: their dances, which are remarkable for their speed and vigour, differ from those of any other group, and years ago they were documented by Cecil Sharpe. Their dress is similarly distinctive and original, consisting of white smocks, brown cord velvet knee breeches, blue stockings, boots, nine bells on leather gaiters strapped to each leg, and black top hats bedecked with flowers and ribbons. The dancers are accompanied by the Foreman or Fool carrying a bladder stick, and they dance to music played on the mouth organ, the fiddle, the concertina, the melodian or the accordian.

Back in June 1877, five Eynsham men – Thomas Buckingham, Thomas Ayers, William Lambourne, William Day and William Evans (all surnames familiar in present-day Eynsham) – were fined 6d. and 10s. 6d. costs each at Witney magistrates' court for 'damaging grass' at Eynsham. They had been practising their morris dancing on grass that was being grown for hay. Two of the men refused to pay and were sent to prison for seven days: since farm workers' wages were most probably about a pound a week at that time, it seems very likely that these two just *couldn't* pay!

At the turn of the century the group was still very active, dancing each Mayday, all through the summer, and again at Christmas time, when they also performed the mumming plays in the village.

They also used to go and dance in front of the big houses in the area at

Christmas. One of their calls was at Blenheim Palace, the home of the Duke and Duchess of Marlborough. One year they were dancing in front of the Duke and Duchess when Ed Russell, who was nicknamed 'Feathers' and played the Fool in the dance troupe, lightly struck the Duchess over the head with his ox bladder, crying cheerfully, 'Good-day Ma'am.' To the surprise of the company, this was all taken in good part by their hosts, who were greatly amused by the sheer personality of 'Feathers' Russell, who was a tall, very striking looking man. He must have impressed the Duke, because in 1902 he commissioned the artist, William Nicholson, who was living in Woodstock at the time, to paint a portrait of 'Feathers' in his morris dancing clothes.

For six or seven consecutive Sundays Ed Russell walked from Eynsham to Woodstock and back, a matter of about ten miles, to have his portrait painted. He was paid good money for each sitting and, in his own words, 'was given a good slap up meal afterwards'; he said it was the easiest money he ever earned in his life. But apparently the money did not do him a lot of good, because when he got back to the village he used to go straight to The Railway Inn, and along with his fellow morris men proceeded to blue the lot. His portrait, 'Chairing the Dancer', was purchased in 1963 for £200 and now hangs in Cecil Sharpe house in London.

When the men were asked how long it took them to learn the dances, one of them said, 'We don't practice very much, we just picks it up.' The group was to go on dancing until the outbreak of the First World War. It re-formed in the 1920s and again in the late 1930s. The side broke up again during the Second World War. After the war, several attempts were made to revive morris dancing in Eynsham, but not until two years ago did this become a reality when Keith Green, a member of an old Eynsham family, successfully formed a new troupe.

And how do I know all this, the reader might ask. Well, just after settling in Eynsham more than thirty-four years ago, one of the first things I did was to join the Women's Institute. I then became a parish councillor for nine years, and at the same time served on a number of village committees. For a long time I helped with the Meals on Wheels service here, and was the hon. organizer of Cancer Research for twenty-eight years.

In this way I met and talked to a great many Eynsham people, many of them elderly and retired; and as I listened to the ways in which some of them had overcome great poverty and led lives of constant hard work and perseverance, which in turn gave them great strength of character, I thought that their way of life, and what they remembered of their childhood and youth in Eynsham, should, in some way, be recorded so that future generations might know what life was like in an English village at the turn of the century and up to and just after the First World War. In *From Acre End* I have allowed my old friends and neighbours to speak for themselves and recreate a world and a community which, alas, has gone for ever.

MOLLIE HARRIS

Eynsham, November 1981.

1 Eynsham Morris Group, 1937 – the only side which did *not* wear the traditional dress.

2 High Street – now called Acre End Street – 1906. Howe's chemist shop and the post office are on the left. The postman with the dog is Albert Dance, the ladies are the telegraphists. Near left is The Swan Hotel; far left, The Railway Inn.

3 Acre End Street, 1910.

The Red Lion Inn is the second building on the left – the cottages next to it have since disappeared. Leonard's Church is in the background. 1910.

Newland Street, 1900. As a child, Ernest Ovenall lived in one of the cottages on the far left. In the background, also on the left, are Burden's the blacksmith, Sawyer's the grocer, and Hiron's the pork butcher.

6 Eynsham High Street in the early 1920s, showing Pimm's grocer's shop on the left, Mumford's gents' hairdressers in the centre, and The Red Lion Inn. In the foreground is the Bartholemew Scho building, in which the old fire engine was kept.

7 Church Street. The baker's van probably belonged to Biggers the baker; the waggon may well hav been unloading flour for Stevens's bakery.

8 Advertising by local tradesmen, all of whom seem to have had more than one string to their bows. The chemist was particularly enterprising with his home-made sauces, perfume, toothache pills and the like. Taken from a parish magazine, 1905.

❧ ANNETTE FAULKNER ❧
née BURDEN

All my childhood I remember the blacksmithing, the men and the great horses and the hot smell that came from the forge. My grandfather, father, brother and uncles, with their shirt sleeves rolled up – big strong arms they all had – and the leather aprons which they always wore.

Such a hive of industry the blacksmith's shop was, with the shoeing of the horses, for horses were used for most every sort of transport. And the farm cart maintenance and the hundred and one jobs a blacksmith did in those days.

The business of Burden's the blacksmith was started by my forbears at least as far back as 1769, and ever since then there has been a Burden blacksmith in Newland Street. It is even said that some of the horses in King Charles I's army were brought to Eynsham to be shod at Burden's, and that was when a battle was being fought at Folly Bridge, Bladon, about three miles from here.

There is evidence all over the old part of the village of the work that the blacksmith did. The weather vane on the church was made by a Burden, as were the iron 'corset' which helps to keep up the old preaching cross in the square, and the railings round it. And there are wrought iron window latches and fasteners, door knockers, letter boxes and even iron window frames with leaden-edged panes, all very much part of the everyday work of the black-smith in the village before the days of automation and mass production.

Besides my grandfather, there were his three sons working for him as well as two sons-in-law. Apart from the shoeing, they made ploughshares and harrows and drags and all manners of things for the farmers. Then there were the iron rims or tyres that they made and fixed on the farm carts, traps and waggons. And, of course, they made all their own horseshoes and nails. These were made in advance and hung on nails on the roof, and some of those horseshoes are still there today. When the owner brought a horse in to be shod, both my grandfather and my father knew at a glance which shoe would fit him.

Some years later, when my grandfather died, my father took over the business and he employed two men regularly; but if he was a bit pushed, my

Uncle Fred, who was also a blacksmith, would come over from Wytham Abbey to give him a hand.

The garden of the house in Newland Street where we lived was very long, and the back yard, the area nearest the blacksmith's shop, which adjoined the house, was used for putting the iron rims round the cart wheels.

As a girl I used to play in the garden a lot, and one day when I and another girl were out there, some boys over in the next garden shouted to us, 'How's yer mother off fer soap?' and I shouted back, 'Up to her ass in lather.' And didn't I get a telling off for that too – you see, my father had heard what I had said. But it was the sort of silly thing that you said in those days, and of course I didn't see any harm in it. And what we were really doing was apeing the older people, because at that time when everybody knew everybody else there was this good-humoured banter whenever folks met. My father's own special greeting to farmers and the like was 'How bist britched?', which really meant 'How much money have you got in your pocket?' And the reply was often, 'Ah not very good, how bist thee?'

And of course in those days the blacksmith's shop was the favourite meeting place for old and young alike. I think that it was the light and warmth that attracted people – specially in wintertime, there was always somebody watching the men at work at the forge. Of course in those days there were no clubs or things like that for the young boys to go to. Another thing was that most of the cottages were very small and nearly everybody had big families, and at night when the father came home there was no room for growing boys round the fire. That's why they were glad to stand round the blacksmith's door for hours, chattering and joking, and, apart from the pubs, it was most likely the warmest place in the village.

There was another blacksmith in the High Street called Rolly Harris. He had lost an eye through getting a piece of metal in it while he was working. My father often got small pieces in his eyes, but thankfully the doctor always managed to get them out.

My father used to say that the blacksmith's and the farrier's trade mark was his leather apron. His own always seemed to be scarred and peeling, but it protected the rest of his clothing. When a horse was shod the blacksmith always worked with his back to the horse, holding the hind leg between his knees resting on the apron, which was split up the centre. First he would remove the old shoe, tossing it onto a heap, along with the old nails. These were later sold for scrap iron. Then he would begin to pare the foot, cutting away or 'parring' any dead bits of hoof. Then he would reach up and take down a horseshoe, which nine times out of ten fitted a treat. He would measure the shoe on the horse, then it would be lifted with tongs and thrust into the red hot forge to be reheated, taken out, and dipped into a tank of water to cool to just the right heat – of course only the blacksmith would know this. It was then again tried on the horse, reheated yet again, slightly cooled and then hammered on the hoof and fixed with nails for a perfect fit.

If a carriage horse or a hunter was brought in to be shod, my father would afterwards paint the hooves around with black paint – this made the horse look very smart. The cart horses were just left as they were. In frosty weather the well-off people brought their horses to have frost nails put in. The ordinary nails would be taken out of the shoes and the frost nails put in their place. These had much thicker heads that protruded from the shoe and so gripped the roads, but the poorer farmers just had their horses shoes 'roughed up' – ridges marked on the horseshoe which served very much the same as the frost nails.

It was a great caper when a young horse was shod for the first time – mostly frightened they were, you see. First the horse would be tied up to a post so that it wouldn't go running off, and a twitch clamped on its mouth, and all the time the young horse would be dancing and francying about, kicking its legs up and swinging its tail. But two or three men would hold him, talking to try and quieten him while he was safely shod.

Of course, all carts, traps and waggons were fitted with iron tyres or rims on the wooden wheels, and because of the rough flint roads in those days these iron rims wore out quickly. It was the blacksmith's job to make and fit new ones. The owners would bring their carts or traps into the blacksmith's shop. The men would take off the wheel and whip off the old tyre, and a new one specially made to size would start to be formed.

Long pieces of iron would first be heated red hot in the forge fire. Then the iron was taken from the forge onto the anvil with huge long tongs, and the men would strike the red hot metal, welding the pieces together to form hoops when cold. Then the tyre was stood on one side while the men made another one. It wasn't economical just to make one tyre, so while the men were at it they went on to make eight or nine in one day. All the hoops then had holes drilled in them by hand for the nails which would keep the rim on the wheel.

Out in the back yard there was a big, tall, narrow oven. It took two or three tyres at a time and was heated with wood. My father used to buy old railway sleepers and have them sawn up to feed the fire. These sleepers were soaked in creosote, so you can imagine how well they burnt up. The fire had to be kept going well all the time because the tyres that had been stacked in the oven had to be absolutely red hot all the way round, and they had to be turned round and round with long tongs all the while to get them in this red hot state all over.

Meanwhile, the wooden wheel that was going to be fitted with a new tyre had been screwed down on to a huge, round iron platform in the back yard. Two men would then whip the red hot tyre out of the oven and drop it on to the wheel, and two or three other fellows went round and round striking the tyre very quickly to get it into position, and all the while another man would be pouring water on to the wheel to stop it from catching fire. They would keep dipping their buckets or watering cans into a big tub to refill them. The water had been drawn up from the old well earlier in the day, ready for this swift operation.

When a wheel was judged to be cool enough, it was stacked to one side, the next one put into place, and the whole procedure repeated again and again. Speed was the great thing, as the remaining tyres in the oven must not get too hot.

The last thing to be done was to drive long nails in the tyres (or rims) to secure them on to the wheel. Then the wheels were passed on to the wheel-wright, Jack Batts, whose yard was just down the road from the blacksmith's, in what is now called Wintle's Farm. The men used to bowl the wheels along, just like children bowled a hoop.

But the great thing after tyring days was the fish feast that followed. My father bought bloaters or herrings, either from Fishy Wright or Mr Pitts, who came on his bike from Woodstock once a week to sell fish in the village. The fish would be put on tin plates and put in the oven. Of course they cooked in no time and we all had a good feed. The locals used to say that the smell wafted all over the village, and folks were heard to remark, 'Ah the black-smith's finished his wheeling, they be on the fish now.'

When my father died, my brother naturally took over the business. But when the First World War broke out he and other village men who were in the Territorials had to go on the first day. So my mother and I managed to keep the business going, with the help of one man who came from Witney three days a week. I used to blow up the fire and hold the knives on the grass mowers while they were sharpened and do all manner of jobs.

Then as soon as the war was over the local farmers got up a petition and got my brother home early.

Of course as the years went by more and more people bought tractors and cars, so the blacksmithing trade of shoeing and tyre-fitting declined. But there was more farm machinery being used, and breaking down. So, as my brother used to say, 'When one door closes another one opens', and he always found plenty to do.

Then at the age of seventy-one, in 1963, my brother retired. His son was a draughtsman, and although he did learn some of the aspects of blacksmithing over the years, he didn't take it up seriously.

For a while the smithy was silent. Then a young man called Peter Kenney rented the forge and building. Of course, its a very different trade to what it was in my father's day. Now decorative wrought iron articles are made there, and with the opening up of the inglenooked fireplaces that were built into the old cottages, fire baskets are in great demand. Recently he was asked to repair the railings round the old cross in the Square which, of course, Burden the blacksmith had made many years ago. So thankfully the old name and the blacksmith's shop live on, although part of the building is now used as a thriving antique shop – run by a member of the Burden family.

9 Mrs Margery Blake – a farmer's wife – and a friend out riding in their pony and trap.

❧ ALICE MAY BATTS ❧
née CLACK *born* 1894

When I was a small child we used to live in one of the farm cottages at a place called the Nunnery, which was part of Twelve Acre Farm at Eynsham, where my dad was employed as a general labourer. But in 1900 we moved to Southleigh, a couple of miles away, and we children went to the village school there. Then I remember the next year we moved again a mile or so up the road to High Cogges where my father was carter to John D. Bury, a big farmer there. We went to Cogges school then.

On Saturdays our mother would send us children into Witney to do some shopping. I reckon it took us all the morning to get there and back – walking of course. Our first call was at the butcher's where I bought a piece of streaky bacon to boil, half a pig's head, some beef suet, some 'seconds' dripping, and some odds and ends of beef, enough to make a boiled pudding for all of us for Sunday dinner. All this cost half-a-crown. This meat would have to last us all the week. Of course in the seasons there were different things that our father caught on the farm which helped to feed us. Always during the springtime the farm workers used to band together and go out at night sparrow catching, with nets. They would fix these over the hedges where they knew the birds were roosting, then bang some tins and the birds would take off but be caught in the nets. Our mother would skin these and cook 'um and we'd have a good feed. Another thing we always had in springtime was rook pie. The farmers used to organize rook shoots and, of course, the farm workers were given some. I remember too the rabbits we used to have – our mother cooked them all sorts of ways, lovely and tasty they was. Ah, and pigeon pie or pigeons in the casserole, we used to have lots of them as well.

Meat wasn't the only thing we bought when we went to Witney shopping. After the butcher's it was down the High Street to 'Fishy Harris's', where we bought seven bloaters for sixpence; if you bought them separately they was a penny each. At that time eggs was fourteen or sixteen for a shilling, and bread 2½d. for a small loaf and 4d. for a big one. I remember buying my brother hobnailed boots for half-a-crown. We girls wore boots as well and they cost the same, but we had what they called 'spriggs' (a type of nail) in ours – they wasn't quite so heavy and rough as the boy's hob-nails. Sometimes our mother asked me to get one of my young sisters a pair of black patent shoes – they had a little strap which fastened with a shoe button, and cost $11\frac{1}{2}d$. We used to buy all our boots from Dingle's in Witney. It was nice to dawdle round the shops, but then there was the long walk home. We was that hungry we used to pick at that suet, then got a cuff round the earhole for eating it. We was very happy as kids. When the chores were done it was outside playing all sorts of games till our mother called us in for bed.

When I was old enough I sat for the labour exam. If you passed it it meant that you could leave school. Well, I passed all right, I'd had my twelve year-old birthday in the December and left school the following Easter.

For the first year I went to live with my dad's sister at Hailey, about three miles away. She had got a young family and I helped her out. Then I came back to High Cogges and went to work for a little while for a Miss Townsend, she kept a small draper's shop in Witney. Then my mother got me a situation in service at a place near Rugby which sounded like the other side of the world to me.

Well, on the Sunday July 11th, before I was due to leave home on the Monday, my father carried my tin box with my bits of clothes in on his shoulder from High Cogges to Eynsham, to Chilbridge Road where my granny lived. He had to do this on the Sunday afternoon as that was the only time he had off, and he had to walk because there was no other way to get there. So the next morning my mother and I set out and walked to Eynsham. We called at Granny's to pick up my tin box, then we caught the train at Eynsham to Oxford, as the mistress that I was going to had provided the train fare for me. When we got to Oxford we had to cross over the road to the L.N.E.R., where I was put in the charge of the railway guard. My mother left me on the platform as she had to get back home and look after my younger brothers and sisters. I stood there waiting for the train to come in which would take me to my destination. My coat, which was one my mother had made from an old one of hers, flapped round my ankles. I had a shilling in one hand and the key for my tin box in the other. I'd never been any more than three miles away from home in my life, and I felt very frightened and lonely.

This job in service that I was going to was a village called North Kilworth near Rugby. This meant that I would have to change trains at Bletchley, where I was again put in the charge of the guard. Well, I got to Rugby station, the guard said 'This is it', and I got off the train and stood waiting on the platform. Gradually all the other people seemed to disappear. I didn't know what to do and I was that hungry 'cos I hadn't had anything to eat

10 Alice May Clack, aged twenty-two, in the
garden of Cogges Priory, where she was
employed as a maid.

since I'd left home at breakfast time and then I'd only had two slices of bread
and dripping.

Then a young gent came up to me and asked me my name. 'Alice May
Clack,' I told him. 'Ah, you are the young person who is going to work for
my mother,' he said. 'I'm sorry I'm late,' he went on, 'but I've been chattering. I'm Mr Whiteman.' He caught hold of the tin box and we went outside
the station and standing out there was a lovely shiny pony and trap. He
helped me up and we were soon off to his mother's house which was only a
few miles away at North Kilworth.

They were ever such nice people to work for and for the first time in my life
I had a room of my own, over the yard, and a lovely soft bed to sleep in, all
on my own too. At home I'd always had to sleep with my sisters. And the
food, it was simply wonderful, I had just the same as my employers. I worked
for Mr and Mrs Whiteman for eighteen months. While I was there I was
confirmed by the Bishop of Peterborough, the Right Revd Carlin. Then I
thought I'd have a change, so I got myself another domestic post just outside
the village on the Leicester Road, at The Grange, working for a Mr and Mrs

Spencer. It was a very good place too, but I didn't seem to have enough to do and I would go and groom the horses and help milk the cows for something to do. Well, once more I thought I'd have a change and go to another post at Claybrook, but I didn't stick that long. It was up in the mornings at five to help with the milking and washing all the dairy stuff, before breakfast too. So on my half day off I walked over to The Grange and asked Mrs Spencer if I could come back and work for her. She said, yes, as long as I didn't make a habit of leaving and each time expect to come back to her.

So I settled down again at The Grange and was very happy. Do you know I didn't go home for five years, not since I set out on the train for Rugby? Then my mistress said that she thought that I should have a holiday. While I was away my mother had three more children, our Doris, Mabel and Albert. Well, my dad met me at Southleigh station and everybody made a good fuss of me, I can tell you.

This was 1915 and my sister Kate was working at the Witney steam laundry and earning well over a pound a week, where I was only getting thirty shillings a month.

Well, I went back to Mrs Spencer at The Grange and gave in my notice and left and went back home and got a job at the laundry. But I didn't like it very much. I worked on a thing they called a calender, like a monstrous mangle it was. It ironed the sheets and table cloths and things in a flash. We girls used to go out into the town at dinner times and buy ourselves a halfpenny bar of chocolate and talk to the soldiers. One day there was a big army convoy going through the town. The great line of soldiers and their equipment stopped for a break and we chatted to those lovely young lads, many of which probably never came back again. Anyhow our vicar, the vicar of Cogges, saw us chatting to these lads and eating our chocolate, and the next Sunday when he saw me at church he said, 'Alice, I do hope that you were not spending your money on riotous living, or going off the straight and narrow.' Honest, what wrong could you do with a halfpenny bar of chocolate and few minutes innocent chatter to some soldiers in Witney High Street, on their way to France?

Then the vicar went on, 'My wife would like to see you, and could you call as soon as possible?' So I went to see Mrs Hugell the vicar's wife, they lived at Cogges Priory, and she asked me if I would go and work for her in the house. Well, I jumped at the chance, because I really did enjoy housework.

I did all the work there, washing, ironing, cooking, waiting at table, cleaned all the house, did the gardening and cleaned the church once a week: for this last work I received an extra £5 a year and I was as happy as a sandboy.

Sometimes on my half day I'd walk over the fields to High Cogges to see my mother and dad and the little ones.

I remember we used to go to St Mary's Church in Witney for evensong during the war, because Cogges church had no blackout. And the vicar used to call us 'Church tramps and parish traitors', only in fun of course.

At this time I was very friendly with my cousin – she worked in service too, for some folk called Fennemore, I think. And I used to spend my holidays with my aunt, this girl's mother, and my uncle who lived in a farmworker's cottage on Twelve Acres Farm in Eynsham where I had lived as a child. Mind you it was only about three miles from my home in High Cogges. Well, that's how I met my husband to be, for he was George Batts, my cousin.

He had joined the army in 1915. He was a despatch rider riding horseback, and once when he was delivering despatches his horse was shot and wounded and he, George, had to shoot the animal out of its misery and continue on foot.

During the war his father died, so he asked his commanding officer if he could go home to the funeral. 'No,' said the officer, 'you can't, there's enough dead lying about here without you going all that way.' He only came home twice during the war. In 1918 he was gassed and wounded and he was awarded the King's Certificate and honourably discharged and invalided out from The Queen's Own Oxfordshire Hussars, and in July 1919 he was awarded a pension of five shillings a week.

We got married in 1920 at Eynsham church, and Swinburn's the bakers at Witney made our wedding cake. By then my husband was employed at Twelve Acre Farm as a carter and we lived in one of the cottages up there. I say up there because its nearly two miles out of Eynsham village. At that time the farm was owned by a Mr Tom Deane.

On the day our first child was born the army stopped my husband's pension, because he didn't go to London to a tribunal. First, he hadn't got the money to go, and another thing he couldn't afford to have the time off from work and lose a day's pay. While we was living up there the Eynsham W.I. was formed and me and my neighbour joined. It was a marvellous thing at that time, somewhere for women to go and mix with other women. We learned all sorts of things at the monthly meetings and looked forward from one month to the next. The road, being a private one, was in a bad state and in the wintertime we used to start off in our wellingtons, then just before we got to the first houses in the village we'd take them off, lay them in the hedge and change into our shoes.

Before we left Twelve Acres we'd got three children.

Then in 1929 my husband went to Wolvercote, just outside Oxford, and bought three horse-drawn trams – the Council was getting rid of them because they were being replaced by motor buses. Well, he set to and built us a lovely bungalow out of these horse trams on a bit of land down the Cassington Road. He even dug his own well so that we could have fresh water. And did you know in the year 1978 Mr Sawyer, who lives near where that bungalow of ours was, opened up the well, which had been covered for safety of cattle, and there was still good fresh spring water in it? My George would have liked to have known that. During that year the doctor said that I was going to have twins and I had to go into Oxford hospital to have them. A boy and a girl, beautiful they were too. I was in there for six weeks, and my mother looked after the children. When they were ten weeks old the boy caught pneumonia and died.

Soon after we moved to a cottage in Newland Street. We hadn't been there long when the Council started to build a second lot of council houses in the village, up Spare Acre Lane or Gas House Lane, as it was sometimes called. We had the chance of one so we jumped at it. A real new house with running water and gas lighting. Later we paid £6 to have the electric light put in.

But the years that followed were very hard. George, my husband, was not in very good health and we'd got five children by then. I used to try and earn a bit of money. When anybody round us had a baby it was 'Go and ask Alice Batts to come and help.' I used to look after the mother and baby, cook, clean and wash for the rest of the family as well as running my own home. I got two and sixpence a day for this. I know it don't sound much now, but them extra few shillings was a godsend, I can tell you.

My husband's health got worse and worse, and his eyesight was bad too. Then after years and years of hard-up-ness, tribunals and medicals and several operations on his eyes, the army agreed that all his bad health, especially the eye trouble, was the result of being so badly gassed during the war. So they gave him a pension and he became a registered disabled. They taught him basket-making and cane work, and folk came from all over the place with broken cane chairs and stools for him to mend. He made hundreds of baskets and stools and the Red Cross supplied him with a nice little workshop as well.

By then we had moved to a council bungalow just up the road a bit and only my youngest son was still at home.

Then some few years later, in 1969, my husband died, December 28th it was, but I soldier on. My family are all very good to me and of course there's the joy of my grandchildren and great-grandchildren.

MARGERY BLAKE
née DEANE *born* 1892

I was born in my present home, which my great-grandfather bought in 1879, and apart from a few years in the late 'twenties and early 'thirties, and while I was away at school for a while, this has been my home.

We lived here, my mother, father, half sister and brother, and my own sister and brother, all one big happy family. When each of us was born, our mother said, Dr Smallhorn had to drive a couple of miles from the village up our stony road in his horse-drawn brougham to attend her.

We three youngest had a governess here in the house to teach us. Every Sunday, wet or fine, we walked down to the village to church with her.

Our father would never allow the ponies and traps to be used on a Sunday. And every day we went for a walk with our governess, usually before tea: we all had a really lovely childhood. We children each had our own small plot in the garden to do and grow what we liked. And we had an aunt who lived at nearby Northleigh who always took us to the pantomime at Oxford at Christmas time. She also took us to St Giles's fair in September, riding there in her lovely horse-drawn brougham, which she drove. She was a very good-looking lady and beautifully dressed, we did feel so important riding with her.

We spent most of the summer swimming in the Thames – down at Pinkhill Lock we went mostly, lifting our bikes over the stiles on our way. Mr Smith, the lock-keeper, lent us an old henhouse to dress and undress in, and I remember we went home covered in hen fleas.

Then, when I was thirteen, I was sent off to boarding school at Reading, just coming home for holidays: my father always met me off the train at Eynsham. I stayed at that school until I was almost eighteen.

Some days I would cycle over to Northleigh to my aunt: it was she who took me to golf and taught me how to play. We played a lot of tennis too, at our farm, sometimes at Dr and Mrs Cruickshanks', at City Farm, and at Bury's at nearby Stanton Harcourt. Lovely social events they were, with the hostess supplying large jugs of cool lemonade, made with real lemons of course.

All my life, it seemed, an elderly man called Freddy Brooks worked for us.

He was the handyman, and such a useful one too. He cleaned all the boots and shoes and the knives and forks and tended the trap pony – well, we called him our groom. He also did the huge garden and grew the most lovely strawberries you ever tasted. His wife used to work for our mother too, in between having babies. She did all sorts of housework and washing, and she reckoned that the stone passages at Twelve Acres were as long as a cricket pitch. I'll bet they seemed that long to her when she had to scrub them weekly on her hands and knees with hot soda water. They lived in a cottage in the rickyard and were a very clean, hardworking family.

There are eight or ten cottages on the farm and in my young days they were all occupied by our farm workers, but with all the modern present day machinery we don't employ a quarter of the staff.

In those far-off days of my youth we had three teams of horses working on the farm, Suffolk punches they were, and most beautiful, magnificent animals. It was marvellous to watch them work. We had a head carter, three under-carters, and three boys to work with them. And shepherds, stockmen, cowmen, and general farm hands.

There were the sheep and cows and pigs to attend to. Of course, the harvest took weeks and weeks to get in, so did the haymaking. And in the wintertime, while some of the men were at plough, others were hedging and ditching. My father took a great pride in the appearance and welfare of the farm.

Then the First World War came along and they took all the men, apart from two very old ones. Some of the fellows who had worked for us were in France within five or six days of leaving the farm, half of them to die in the trenches there. We who were left behind at Twelve Acres had an awful time. My father fell ill, then my sister had T.B. Poor George Batts was on a rick helping with the threshing one morning, and he was dead that same night. This was during the dreadful 'flu epidemic, and people died like flies. Afterwards we realized how ill Mr Batts must have felt on that morning up on the rick – but in those days it was a case of 'no work, no pay', and they had a large family, and I suppose the poor man couldn't afford to stop away from work.

I worked very hard during that awful war, I reckon I did a full day's work in the house, and then another day's work in the evening in the garden. Somehow I seemed to regain my strength out in that vast garden on those lovely cool summer evenings, with the smell of the dew, damp on the 'nearly ready to cart' hay in the fields which surrounded the farm – funny how you remember little things like that.

Sometimes I drove my mother in the pony and trap to Witney to do some

11 The two young Miss Deanes, whose father owned Twelve Acre Farm. After her father's death, the little girl on the bottom step married Gordon Blake, and returned to live at Twelve Acres.

shopping, going along the old right of way, through to Southleigh and then on to the town. And in the summertime we walked along the same right of way or bridlepath to Southleigh church to evensong. Beautiful evenings full of birdsong, scurrying rabbits and the sweet, sweet smell of the countryside.

Then in 1922 my father died, and my mother went to Devon to live (she didn't care for Oxfordshire). I went to Northleigh, three miles away to my aunt's and lived there for a while. Meanwhile my half-brother farmed Twelve Acres. But this was during the terrible slump, and in the end he lost all his money. Then Mrs Cruickshank, the doctor's wife, introduced me to the young man who was to become my husband – Gordon R. Blake, a civil servant who worked at Somerset House.

Soon we were married, and in 1933 we came back to Twelve Acres to live. By then we had got two children, one three-and-a-half and the other eighteen months. My husband continued to work as a civil servant and put a good manager in to run the farm; but all the while, in his spare time, my husband learned all he could about farming. He took a great interest in village life, serving on one committee and another. But I didn't ever seem to have any time to spare for that sort of thing.

During the early years of our marriage most of my time was spent in bringing up the children, helping with the farm accounts and working in my beloved garden. Then the time came for the children to go to school. They went off to Witney on the bus for the first few years; later, during the Second World War, they both attended schools in Oxford, my daughter at Oxford High School and my son at the Dragon School. When many of the buses were stopped during the war, the children used to often go part of the way on the milk waggon, picking up a bus near the city.

And because Twelve Acres was such a big house I had to have several women and children billeted on me early on in the war. They had to sleep on mattresses on the floor, and all the husbands came at the weekends. The women couldn't settle to our quiet life in the country, especially as the farm was two miles from the nearest shop, and gradually they all went back to their homes in Battersea.

Then we had several prisoners of war sent to help do the farm work. The Germans came first, then the Italians. The Germans were very nice fellows, very hard working too. One called Zolner, I remember, had frostbite in both legs and after he left the farm we heard that he had to have both legs off. While they were with us the prisoners lived in what we called the lower cottages or the Nunnery cottages. The men had to fend for themselves, but I used to do their shopping for them, collecting their ration cards from a

12 Corn drilling with two horses at Twelve Acre Farm.

13 One of the first steam ploughs in the area.

building in Beaumont Street in Oxford and buying their meat and rations in the market. They were very clever men and in their spare time carved the most lovely toys from bits of wood, which they sold to the locals. I even had to purchase their cigarettes for them.

Since the war there have been many changes and several incidents on the farm. For years we had our own water supply – the huge water tanks were very near the farmhouse, great tanks holding 130,000 gallons. The building had a thatched roof; one day it caught fire, and the farm workers put the fire out. We then had to call in the local fire brigade to pump all the water out as the tanks were full of burnt straw.

The water was pumped up by a 'windmill' type pump which eventually blew down in a severe gale. Two more boreholes were dug in different parts of the farm, but each time the 'powers that be' turned them down as unfit for animal or human use. Apparently the water held a large percentage of Glauber salts – no wonder we could get no fat on the pigs! And we are plagued with rooks here, always building in the chimney pots they are. We have had sheep stolen out of the fields: once our farm foreman was coming back to work at dinnertime and he actually met two men in a van with some of our sheep in the back. He turned round, chased and caught them, then handed them over to the police.

At one period my husband went in for turkey rearing – thousands of day-old chicks we packed in boxes and sent off all over the country, mostly by rail. Then at Christmas time we sold hundreds of full-grown ones, many of them going to Oxford market. But always keeping most of the land planted with corn and grass for the big milk herds and the sheep.

Then the dreaded Dutch Elm disease struck, especially here in Oxford-shire. There were three hundred elm trees on our six hundred acres on the farm – all those will have to come down. My husband, whose health had deteriorated over the past two years, died last autumn. My son, who farms a few miles away, and a farm foreman now runs Twelve Acres. I still live in this huge house, but I have a good companion and my children are near. My son does not want to own this farm – he is quite settled where he is – but I would like to think that his young son might come and take over here one day, when he is old enough.

❧ ERNEST WILLIAM OVENALL ❧
born 1893

We came to Eynsham – my mother, brothers and sister and I – in 1902, because of a smallpox epidemic at Purfleet, Essex. My father, who was an engineer in the Anglo-American Oil Works, had just died of smallpox. I was the eldest of five and just nine years old. We went to live next door to granny, she at 5 Newland Street and we at 6, and we lived there for twelve years. My mother paid 3*s*. 6*d*. a week rent, and not a penny was spent on the cottage during that time.

There were two rooms up and two down and a big pantry, but my granny had three up and two down, so I used to sleep in hers. All the cottages in our row had window shutters which were closed at night and fastened from the inside with a short bolt and pin. They served two purposes: first, no window blind was needed and second, in the winter, they helped to keep the room warm. My mother used to buy a hundredweight of coal each week and it cost a shilling. We had a wide windowsill inside, and we always had a window full of geraniums and pelargoniums. They made a good show from the outside, but kept out a lot of daylight. There was no wallpaper on the walls – mostly they were lime-washed white or pale blue and the ceilings were white too. The lighting was by candle or paraffin oil lamps. The lamp was usually hung on a nail on the wall. Some people had table lamps with a shade which they placed on the table when lit. Our furniture was very plain – a deal table which had to be scrubbed, and chairs of the Windsor type. We had no easy chairs. There was a chest of drawers, and a picture or two on the walls, some depicting scenes from the Bible.

The floors were laid with stone slabs, which were very cold to the feet. Parts of the floor were covered with rag rugs which everybody made from old clothes cut into strips and pegged on to a hessian sack. About once a week the stone floors were scrubbed. The beds were of lathe type, with straw palliasses with a flock bed on the top.

The fireplace in the living room had two hobs on. One side was a very small hot water tank, and the other an oven. All the cooking was done on this fire – only the better class houses had gas stoves and gas lighting at this time. The space in the fire grate was about 12 or 15 inches above the floor level, and a 'tidy' or dust preventer stood on the hearth in front of the space below the fire and kept falling cinders or ashes from spreading all over the hearth, which our mother whitened daily with a 'hearthstone'. In front of the hearth was a steel fender kept bright with emery cloth. The black parts of the grate were kept blackleaded. On the fender were laid the fire-irons, again made of steel and consisting of a poker, tongs and a shovel. A pair of bellows was there to be used to help a slow fire burn. Puddings and stews were often cooked in the oven, and sometimes my mother used a Dutch oven which she hooked on the front bars of the fire. Some people had bread ovens. Nearly all the cottagers took their Sunday roast to one of the village bakers to be cooked.

We had a lean-to back scullery where all the washing was done by hand. We had to get our water from a stand-pipe in the yard – you had to pay an extra sixpence a week if the tap was indoors in the back scullery. The water was heated up in a copper which stood in the corner of the room. Most folk burned slack coal and any bits of kindling wood to heat up the water. The only aids my mother had were a packet of soda and a big bar of yellow washing soap. My gran had a big wooden mangle that she used to get the 'water-wet', as she called it, out of the sheets and things. After the washing was dry, or nearly so, it was ironed. This was done by flat irons. These were made of iron with a smooth face: the shape was roughly similar to the present day electric iron, but it was made entirely of iron and when hot was held in a cloth holder. The irons were heated by placing them on a bracket with hooks which were hooked over the front bars of a bright coal fire. When the irons were considered hot enough they were rubbed by a cloth to make sure they had not been sooted by the fire. Two irons were generally in use and they were used alternately: when the one in use cooled off it was replaced on the bracket in front of the fire and the other one used, and so on until the ironing was completed. How my mother managed I don't know. We had parish relief – five shillings a week and two big loaves. This was granted by the Essex Council, and it was them who insisted that I stayed at school until I was fourteen, the usual age at that time was thirteen, because I had lost so much schooling because of the smallpox at Purfleet.

In the summer the roads in the village were very dusty when the wind blew, but in the winter they were covered with mud. Men were employed to scrape it off with mud scrapers; they would then load it into carts and take it away and tip it on a dump, or on the side of a country road.

There was one doctor in Eynsham, who also attended patients in some of the other nearby villages. Whether you called him in or went to see him, the

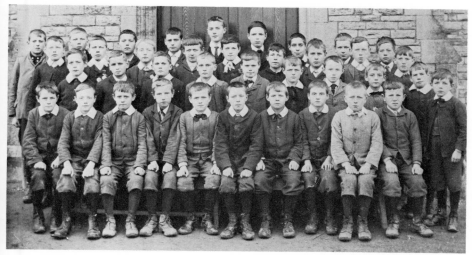

14 Board School photograph, 1907. Second from the left, back row, is Ernest Ovenall; second on the left, third row, is his brother, Albert Ovenall, wearing medals for good attendance. Centre back row is Maurice Blake, who later started the 'pop' factory; the boy on his right, J. Burden, became the village blacksmith.

15 Mr Trethewy, the headmaster of the Board School from the turn of the century to the early 1920s. Strict but fair, he had a great influence on his pupils.

16 The medals which were given to Ernest Ovenall for good attendance at school.

patient had to pay for the doctor's services. No ambulances were available, and urgent cases had to make their own way to the hospital by borrowing a pony and cart from one of the bakers. The villagers paid a shilling per year for the services of a district nurse.

There were no telephones then, only the telegraph at the post office. It cost sixpence for twelve words to send a telegram, a penny to post a letter, and a halfpenny for postcards.

There were three schools in the village – the National School in Station Road for infants, the Board School in Witney Road for older children, and Miss Swann's little private school in Redthorn House on the corner of Mill Street and Newland Street.

Mr Trethewy was the schoolmaster at the Board School, and a very good man he was too. At that time the education authorities awarded medals for regular attendance and good conduct, and we were very proud when we were awarded one of these. During 1906–7 the education authorities took a very important decision. They decided to drop the teaching of algebra and put the decimal system in its place. That was a big mistake as far as I was concerned, because it's impossible to advance in maths without a thorough understanding of algebra. One day we had been having lessons about proportions, ratios, interest, percentages, and stocks and shares. Going home from school I stopped to chat to a gardener, Arthur Green, and being keen on the lesson we'd had, I started to tell him about it, quoting all the subjects. He listened very patiently to me and then remarked, 'I don't know all about them stocks and shares my boy, but I do know about stocks and asters.'

There were not many school books, and things like poetry were taught from the blackboard. The teacher would write down a verse at a time and then we would have a certain time to memorize it. So too with things like timetables and weights and measures. I think being taught like this you always remember.

During my schooldays I got a job as houseboy to a Mr Arthur Blake who lived at that big house in Queen Street, The Gables. I used to go there at eight o'clock in the morning before school, then at dinner time and after school. I used to have to clean the knives and forks with a knifeboard and brick dust, and I had to run all the errands too. Another job was pumping water up to a tank from an artesian well, this alone took me half an hour. *For all this I was paid sixpence a week.*

There were no playing fields in my school days, just the playground which had yellow gravel over it. There were no washbasins or anything like that and the only drink you could get was from the water tap in the playground.

I don't remember a drinking cup, we just used to put our heads under and drink direct from the tap. Once Mr Trethewy gave me a penny, I think I'd done an errand for him, but he handed me a half-crown by mistake, so I handed it back to him and he gave me a penny back, without a word. The next day we had a lecture from him and the subject was honesty. Another time Frank Sawyer sent me to Mr Gibbon's shop in Lombard Street to get a pound of sausages which cost sixpence. I asked Mrs Gibbons for them, she handed them to me, took the sixpence and was just putting it in the till when her husband Mr Gibbons came in. He said, 'Look, that's a half sovereign he's given you,' and handed me the change. When I got back and handed Mr Sawyer the change he was surprised as I was. He and I and Mrs Gibbons had thought it was a sixpence.

One year there was a big epidemic of measles and nearly all the children in the village went down with it. All we five children had it and it left us all very pale and weak. So one sunny September afternoon our mother thought she'd take us for a walk in the fresh air. She packed a bit of food and a bottle of water in a basket, and we set off for Swinford, and then walked to the top of Beacon Hill about a mile out of the village. We had a lovely time up there. Then we picked some blackberries and found a few mushrooms and put them in the basket and then we set off for home. On the way back we were challenged by a keeper who said to mother 'What's in that basket?' He snatched it from her hand, looked inside and then tipped the contents on the ground and stamped on them, saying 'Now clear off.' My mother had a job to hold back the tears, I can tell you. But life wasn't all sadness, and it had its brighter moments. One night just before Mr Hall the baker closed his shop, I went in and asked for a pennyworth of stale cakes. 'Well,' Mr Hall said, 'We haven't got any stale cakes today, but they will be by tomorrow,' and he handed me a bag full. Trying to ward off thieves, Mr Hall had these words pinned up in his shop:

> He as steals what is'nt issen
> When he's copped he goes to prison.

There was no dentist in the village when I was young and of course no national health, so any treatment had to be paid by the patient. I had toothache something terrible, so my mother took me down to the surgery to Dr Cruickshank and he took my tooth out with a pair of forceps. There was no question of an injection to kill the pain – you had to just 'grin and bear it'.

We children used to go to Sunday School at the Baptist chapel, and we belonged to the Band of Hope. These meetings were held in the Baptist schoolroom at the back of the chapel, and once a year all the Bands of Hope for miles around used to assemble in the quadrangle at Blenheim Palace on August Bank Holiday Monday. We used to be issued with a card and we paid a halfpenny a week until we had saved $6\frac{1}{2}d$. We were taken to Blenheim Palace in a wagonette and we had a wonderful tea: there were hundreds of children there. We played organized games and it always seemed to be a hot sunny day.

On Sunday mornings in the summer we used to walk down Mead Lane and across the fields and railway lines to the Paddles, the village bathing place. It was not in the Thames but in a nearby stream, called the Nates by the locals, which had earlier been the canal to the wharf by The Talbot Inn. There were as many as forty boys and young men there: besides swimming and bathing there were races across the fields and, in several places, across the stream.

Of course we youngsters couldn't swim and nobody bothered to teach us – it was a case of every man and boy for himself. What we did was to cut bullrushes from the stream, weave and bind them together, and make a small raft, about two foot wide. These we slipped under our chests and they kept us afloat until we felt we had conquered the art of swimming.

Then it was back to the village and to 'Whitlocks' the bakers in Mill Street to fetch the Sunday dinner which had been taken earlier for Mr Whitlock to cook in the bread oven. It was always beautifully done, and cost $1\frac{1}{2}d$. for cooking. In the afternoon we usually went to the chapel for Bible class for an hour. After tea in the evening we would walk down to the railway station to see the train draw in at 7.30 p.m. for Oxford and the passengers who left by it after visiting their friends in the village over the weekend.

When I left school I got a job at Mr Frank Sawyer's. I had to deliver newspapers and milk and help to mind the shop, and every night I had to scrub the shop floor after we closed. Mr Sawyer would bring me three buckets of clean water for this. The milk I took round the village in a two-gallon can. The milk was measured out to the customer by hap'orths ($\frac{1}{2}d$.) and pen'orths ($1d$.) into jugs or basins. The measure was dipped into the big can: there were quarter-, half- and one-pint dippers. After the milk delivery 'twas the paper round. I used to have to ride an old cushion-tyred bike, although pneumatic ones were in use by then. We called this old shop bike the Boneshaker. As well as the village I had to go to other nearby villages, Church Hanborough, Long Hanborough, Freeland and Barnard Gate, and get back home at dinner time. And mind the shop in the afternoon. All this for $3s.$ $6d.$ a week – and I stayed there until I was sixteen, and worked seventy-two hours a

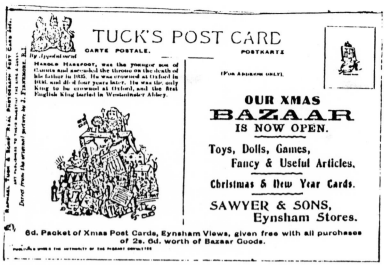

17 The postcard delivered round the village by Sawyer & Sons, just before Christmas 1910. A sixpenny packet of postcards of views of Eynsham was given free with all purchases from the bazaar worth 2s. 6d. or more.

week. Then I took a job as a postboy with Mr Howe who kept the post office and was also chemist to the village. To get this trustworthy job I had to walk with Dick Tredwell, another postman, to Southleigh to a magistrate to be sworn in, as it were. We went on the footpath via Twelve Acre Farm, along an old right of way. This was not so far as walking along the main road to Southleigh: even so, it was about four miles. My first job every day was to meet the mail at six o'clock in the morning. This was brought in a mail cart from Oxford in a horse and trap. Mr Howe the postmaster was well over sixty at the time, but was always up to sort the mail. I delivered letters to Swinford (and cleared the letter box there), Stroud Court, Pinkhill Lock, and then over the river – I fell in more than once on slippery mornings – to Pinkhill farm, then back across the fields. Course I had to push my bike much of the way.

After that it was back to work in the shop. We should have finished work at 7.15 pm, but I had to stay till eight in case there were any messages (telegrams) to deliver.

The messages came by Morse code. There was a real delivery boy, but he left at 7.15 because of his age. Then I was on duty every other Sunday for two hours and got a cup of cold coffee for it. The pay was six shillings a week for eighty-two hours. But it was a good job and we had our laughs. One little jingle that we made up at the time included the names of some of the folk who worked there. You see, the postmaster's name was *Howe*. Two of the

18 The staff of the post office. *Back row, left to right:* Herbert Evans, Risby Coombs, Teddy Smith, Chris Brooks. *Front row:* Albert Dance, Alfred Howe (postmaster), postman Barson.

postmen were called *Coomb* and *Dance*. The messenger boy was called *Cox*, the telegraphists Hilda *Cox* and Mrs *Dickens*. So we used to chant: *Howe the Dickens can the Cox Coomb Dance?*

I started to save a bit of money then. I used to buy a penny stamp a week: when you'd got twelve on a card, it was then transferred to a post office bank book. As I said, Hilda Cox was the telegraphist and was paid five shillings a week, but she got the sack and went to the postmaster in Oxford, had a test, and got a better job at a guinea a week.

One evening a telegraph message came in for a person at Worton, a hamlet about four and a half miles away. The postmaster said to me, 'If you will take it tonight I'll give you tenpence.' Mind you there was six inches of snow on the roads. Well, tenpence was a lot of money, so I called at home for my brother, for company, and we set off in a snowstorm, to Cassington, then on to Worton – for tenpence.

Then I saw an advertisement in the paper – 'Wanted, youths to deliver goods for Sainsbury's in Oxford'. So off I went and got a job, riding solid-tyred bikes or a box tricycle for twelve shillings a week. The hours were Mondays, Tuesdays and Wednesdays 7 am till 7.30 pm, Thursdays 7 am till 1.30 pm, Fridays 7 am till 8.30 pm, and Saturdays 7 am till 10.30 pm. There were no holidays apart from the usual bank holidays, and no paid overtime.

I was given two white jackets which had to be laundered at our own expense at a cost of tuppence a week. Of course it meant a very long day because I had to bike into Oxford first and the roads were in a terrible condition. We errand boys parked our bikes in a stable in the Clarendon Hotel yard in Cornmarket. After a while I told the manager I couldn't manage on twelve shillings a week as sometimes in the very bad weather I had to lodge in Oxford for the night, so he gave me a rise of two shillings. But those solid-tyred bikes were awful to ride – it was a job to stay on them, what with the tram lines and cobbled streets in Oxford, and all the jarring about used to break the eggs something terrible, and the manager was always grumbling at us for this.

My mother was glad of any financial help that I could give her. As it was, she had to go out washing in well-off folks' houses. She always did the Swanns' washing – they were a big family who lived at Redthorn House, where the private school was. My mother used to be washing all day Monday there, then she had to bring it all home and iron it – all for two shillings. My gran used to take in washing as well – quite a few people earned themselves a few coppers in this way.

One winter, Mr Trethewy started an evening class for arithmetic, in the old Bartholomew schoolroom in the Square. There was no charge for this – I expect he realized that most of us who had been to the Board School really needed a bit more learning if we were to get on in the world. It was on a Thursday night, so I used to go, as that was my half-day off from Sainsbury's.

In 1910 I came back to the village to work for Mr Edgar Sawyer, brother to Frank who I'd worked for when I first left school. At that time these two brothers ran two separate shops, but later on it became one village shop. Edgar Sawyer's was a grocery, ironmonger, furniture and general hardware. Again the hours were very long, but I did get paid thirteen shillings a week. I had to tend the pony and drive it with a trap to deliver goods in the surrounding villages and help to serve in the shop. One of my jobs while I was working there was to make ha'penny screws. These were made from pieces of newspaper, about five inches square. You took hold of a corner of the paper by the right hand and the opposite corner in your left, gave it a twist and made a little three-cornered bag. The bottom end you sealed by giving it a twist, and into these ha'penny bags or twists I put a small handful of broken biscuits, then tucked the little flap in so that the contents couldn't fall out. Mr Sawyer could buy tins and tea chests full of broken biscuits cheaply from Huntley and Palmers, the big biscuit firm at Reading. The village children used to go mad on them – course first you had to acquire a

[47]

ha'penny. I can remember when I was younger our mother would buy us children one each as a treat, and we got very excited if we found a bit of pink and white wafer or half a cream filled biscuit in our ha'penny twist.

Another job I had was to fill pint bottles with paraffin oil. It was only a penny a pint, but that was how the poor folk bought it, a pint at a time. Course the better off people bought a gallon for eightpence.

I stuck at this job till 1912, then on the spur of the moment packed it up. My mother was worried and said 'Whatever shall we do now?' So I said to her, 'I'm off to see Uncle Fred tomorrow, he said he would always find me a job.' My uncle lived at Dudley in Worcestershire. My mother never tried to stop me, but just said, 'I'd better get out your clean shirt then.' Next morning I was up early. My bit of luggage was a small tin box which I strapped on the back of my bike and started off for Dudley at half-past seven. I got to Bladon (four miles from home) and the pedal came off my bike. I wondered if this was an omen, to go back. Anyhow there was a bike shop in Bladon, so I sat on the path and waited for it to open, bought a new pedal and fixed it on, and was off on my way again. I got as far as Warwick and knocked a woman off her bike and we both landed in the ditch. Neither of us was hurt but the forks of my bike were twisted. Anyhow I went on my way and got to Dudley at four o'clock; that was seventy-five miles I'd biked. My uncle worked on the railway and he got me a job there, loading and unloading goods, the hardest job I ever had in my life that was. The hours were seven in the morning till six at night, for a pound a week. I stopped there for eighteen months. When I was twenty I got a job at the Post Office on telephones. And I thought that was my job for life. In 1913 the engineers could see what a future there was in telephones and arranged classes for us youngsters at Birmingham. When I qualified I got my City and Guilds Certificate and an extra shilling a week. By then I was earning good money, twenty-five shillings a week. Mind you, I always sent a bit of money home to my mother. After a bit I was put on maintenance work. There was a battery in every telephone, a wet battery with two cells which had to be cleaned and filled up with sal ammoniac and water, carbon plates and zinc rods.

In 1916 I was tested for the army under the 'Lord Derby' scheme. I passed A.1, but was not released at that time by the Post Office because of the important work I was doing.

Then in 1918 I joined up, in the Royal Engineers – course the war was nearly over then. We were sent out to Egypt, our officer told us that it was a trip of a lifetime for us, and it was too. We saw all the sights – the Pyramids, Sphinx, etc. We saw Cleopatra's Needle in the middle of some sugar cane fields.

19 Ernest Ovenall in army uniform, with the young lady who was to become his wife; probably taken in 1918.

After that I was demobbed and got married and settled down. Back in civvy street I started work on the telephones at Stourbridge, then on to Dudley which was one of the three places in the country which had automatic exchanges installed, known as 'the Western Electric Rotary Automatic System'. Then I was put in charge of all the automatic equipment at Fort Dunlop – you know, the tyre place. I was there till about 1928.

Then I got involved in the first automatic telephone exchanges in Birmingham, which was ultimately to take 10,000 lines. Course I was still going to technical classes, and I got my final City and Guilds certificates. And that qualification made me an Associate Member of the Institute of Electrical Engineers, so now I could put A.M.I.E. after my name.

I stayed at my job until I was sixty-five, then retired and came back to the village. I've been retired over twenty years now – my interests are home-made wine-making, local history and chatting to old friends.

❧ IDA MILLICENT GREEN ❧
née BIGGERS *born* 1901

I was born in the High Street, where the baking business is still carried on. But before this, in 1889, my parents lived at 63 Mill Street [where the author now lives], where my eldest brother and sister were born. This was where my father started up as a baker. He was by trade a carpenter, but took the baking from a man who had lived at 63 Mill Street and used to keep a pet fox there. My father made an oak wheel barrow which was used to deliver the bread round the village. When it rained a thick flour sack would be thrown over the loaves. Later on, when they moved to High Street, he had a horse and cart – well in the end he had two, one for bread delivery and one for coal. Later on my parents also sold pig and chicken food and had a small grocer's shop, as well as the bakers and the coal business. Best coal at that time was $4\frac{1}{2}d$. a quarter of a hundredweight. Our mother used to tell us about one young lad who worked for them. He was asked to deliver a quarter of a hundredweight of cheap coal, costing $3d.$, to a house in Chapel Yard, which he did. The woman complained and said that no coal had been delivered, but what the lad had done was go into the cottage and put it straight on the woman's fire.

I remember the long hours put in by my father and the man who used to work for him. And these are my memories of the life of a baker before the First World War.

When the flour was delivered, the sacks weighing two-and-a-quarter hundredweight were carried on the men's backs to a loft up the very selfsame ladder that is in the yard to this day. When required for bread-making, these sacks of flour had to be carried down again.

In the bakehouse were two large wooden bins stretching the whole length of the bakehouse – one bin on each side. Each bin was divided into two, one half being filled with flour to reach room temperature, the other half being used to mix the previous day's flour into bread. The other bin was similarly used for the second batch of bread to be made up later in the day.

Pig potatoes were bought by the sack. When they were required they were scoured with a broom, put into huge wooden tubs, covered with water and put into the bakehouse oven till cooked. They were then put through a sieve

20 The Biggers family. Ida Biggers – later Ida Millicent Green – is the little girl in a basket chair to the left of the picture.

to remove most of the skin, thoroughly mashed with a very large wooden club (for the want of a better word), and then mixed in with the flour. When we were young, Sunday night was the only night of the week that we were up late enough to go into the bakehouse and ask for a few of these potatoes to eat. How delightful they were too!

Huge cast-iron boilers were filled with water and put into the oven for some hours before the dough was made. Some of this water was used to mix the salt and yeast together. The temperature had to be 78°. How they knew the correct temperature I don't know – it must have been guesswork. This was poured, several gallons at a time, into the flour, which was then mixed laboriously by hand. It took ages to get the dough to the right consistency. This dough was then covered for the night, and left. The first thing the baker had to do when he came at 5 am next morning was to light the fire and the flue with straw and coal to get the oven hot.

The baker proceeded to knead the dough thoroughly. Then he had to lift it in large lumps across the bakehouse to the top of the other bin, where he would weigh it in either 2 lb 2 oz or 4 lb 4 oz, the extra 2 oz being allowed for wastage in cooking. Each loaf would be moulded by hand, the bottom half of a cottage loaf in one hand and the top of the loaf in the other, simultaneously. Apparently only two shapes of bread were made then, cottage and coburg. These were sold at $2\frac{1}{4}d$. and $4\frac{1}{2}d$. respectively. Once a week dough cakes were baked, but not many people could afford them.

The loaves were then put into the oven with wooden peels or bakers' shovels similar to the ones used today. To see if the bread was cooked a small lamp was used – like Aladdin's magic lamp, containing lard and a wick. As the oven was gradually emptied this lamp was pushed further in until all the loaves were out. The bread then had to be carried out to the cart to which the horse had been harnessed, ready to deliver the bread, which in most cases was not paid for until the end of the week, and sometimes not then.

Outlying villages such as Cassington and Yarnton were supplied too. My brother remembers delivering bread at 10 o'clock at night to people in Cassington who were already in bed – a tin box was left for him to put the loaves in. He remembers that at one house he used to leave sixteen loaves on a Saturday.

Every Friday a relieving officer used to come to the bakehouse. The poor people of the village used to line up in the yard for a large loaf, and sometimes a shilling as well, which he used to dole out. Of course if they had any visible means of sustenance they were not given anything.

There was one woman who had been reported to the relieving officer as having several 'little pigs'. These, of course, could be sold to bring her in some money. When the officer tackled her about this she said, 'If you believe that you call at our house to see them.' This he did, to be confronted with her 'little pigs' (children) sitting round her table waiting for a meal.

Although we lived at the bakehouse in the High Street, we still kept some land at the back of 63 Mill Street, called The Close. On this land we kept lots of pigs. In those days they were only slaughtered in the wintertime. Harry our baker used to come and kill them. He used to tie the pigs' legs together and he and another man would flop them on to a big wooden stool. Then Harry used to 'stick the pig' and the blood used to ooze out. When the pig was dead they would lift it on to a bolton of lighted straw to burn off the bristles. Then he'd take the toenails out and give them to us to suck – they were lovely. Fresh pigmeat would then be sold to customers. Our mother would sell the head for fourpence. But the hams were kept. My mother used to salt them in a lead-lined trough. Christmas didn't seem like Christmas if we didn't have a 26 lb ham on the table. My dad used to cut off all the fat, and Harry our baker used to take it home.

21 John Biggers, whose father founded the bakery, with probably their first motorized delivery van.

Always on Boxing Day, when we were young, the mummers used to come into our yard and perform. We loved this.

We children always went to Sunday School and the Band of Hope, and we used to go to a service of songs and stories which was our entertainment. But there were many poor folk about and one woman used to come in mother's shop for one penny Oxo and a ha'penny candle.

In 1905, when my eldest brother, John, was fourteen years old, he had pneumonia, and he had to have an operation in our house. He had a tube in his body for draining. The trained nurse who was supposed to be looking after him let him walk downstairs one day, the tube went into his body, and he died.

When I was eleven years old I won a scholarship to go to Milham Ford School in Oxford and I stayed there till I was eighteen. I took a teaching job at Eynsham, and then went on to Stanton Harcourt three miles away and stayed there till I retired. In 1937 my father died and my brother Chris took over the baking business. Now I help serve in the bakehouse shop for a few hours most days. Chris's son Arthur runs the firm of Biggers's bakery these days. Now they bake eight different types of white loaves, beside wholemeal, stone-ground and brown, and a wonderful selection of all sorts of cream and fancy cakes and wedding cakes, and they still use the same brick-built oven that my father put in when he first started in the High Street in 1900.

♫ ERNEST EDWARD HARRIS ♫

born 1901

My first memories are of going to the Infants' School in Swan Lane in 1906. Miss Goodwin was our teacher and we used to act little plays, specially at Christmas time. I reckon I was about five years old when we did one little play called *The Brave Coal Miners*. We was all dressed up as coalminers with blackened faces and we carried cardboard lanterns and pickaxes, walking on to the makeshift stage in school singing –

> We are jolly black miners
> As happy as can be
> We work underground
> And there's none as happy as we.

But I was far too bright and much more advanced than the rest of the children, and instead of encouraging me I was often punished for answering the teacher before she finished asking the questions.

It was the same when I moved up to the big school, and one teacher, Miss Anderson, was for ever rapping me on the knuckles just because I answered up too quick.

And when I moved up to Mr Pratt's class it was worse than ever – mind you, I used to play him up something awful. One day he got me in a temper and I socked him one and knocked two of his teeth out, and he tried to stop me and he nearly choked me with my coat collar. I was only twelve and they expelled me from school for that. But the parson patted me on the back, gave me tuppence and said to me 'You should go far, my son.'

My parents were the local carriers, and both my mother and father worked hard driving the horse and carrier's cart into Oxford four times a week, taking passengers for tuppence a time and taking and bringing all manner of things for the villagers – groceries from Grimbly Hughes the wholesalers for the shops in Eynsham, women's clothes, boots on appro., chickens from the market, bikes, in fact anything that was wanted.

From the Maple Dairy in Oxford my parents would buy what was advertised as 'double weight margarine' boxes of one pound for a shilling and the other free. They also bought great sides of bacon covered in big sacking wrappers, which they sold for 2s. 2d. a pound. And on Thursdays they always went in the carrier's cart to Witney because it was market day, or 'hurdle Thursday' as the locals called it, because the hurdle pens were put up in the market square to hold the sheep that the farmers brought in to be sold. They also bought eggs at ninepence a dozen, brought them back to Eynsham, and sold them the next day to the villagers for a shilling a dozen.

As soon as I was old enough I helped with the business, hitching up the horse to the carrier's cart for my father and helping to deliver and collect goods. Always on a Saturday night we collected parcels of meat from Robert Alden in the market in Oxford. These were gifts for the poor folk in Eynsham, and they used to wait for us to drive into the Square at night. You should have seen their faces when we handed out them parcels of meat. You see the Aldens was big chapel folk, and came to the village every Sunday to preach.

We also kept a lot of pigs too which we slaughtered, and sold out the pigmeat to the villagers. We would say 'Ah, Charlie the butcher's coming tomorrow' when we were going to have some killed. Folks never killed their pigs until they was twenty score or more – the old men would gaze over the sty at an animal and say 'Ah, 'e ent ripe yet' if they thought a pig hadn't reached twenty score.

About this time my father bought three cottages in Trapp Alley for £650 for the three, and one of my jobs was to collect the rents every week. Two was let at three shillings a week and the other one at half-a-crown, and old Harriet, who lived in the half-a-crown one, would bring her rent along sometimes, always at mealtimes mind you. Well, our mother couldn't see her standing there while they ate their dinner, so she would ask old Harriet to share their meal, and sometimes the old gel would eat more than her week's rent was worth.

In them days the old men would send you off to the pub to get them a bottle of beer, there was a paper seal on the top of the bottle which must not be broken, otherwise the old men would accuse you of taking a sip. 'Twas tuppence a pint then, you could get an ounce of baccy, a box of matches and a pint of ale for sixpence. If the old men didn't want matches, then you had the farthing change for going.

There was lots of little shops about all over the village, in the front rooms of the cottages mostly. Billy Barton kept a little sweet and tobacco shop in one of the Jubilee cottages. Well, from his shop the old men could buy a clay pipe, filled with baccy – called 'a pipe and a draw' – for a halfpenny. It upset the parson because Billy would sell things on a Sunday, so the parson saw to it that Billy was fined for opening his shop on the sabbath. Billy told them 'I got no money to pay the fine', so they took goods out of his little shop up to the value of the fine.

One day we boys was messing about in Saunders's farmyard and we starts playing with what the farmer called 'a Banbury turnip cutter'. This was a machine like an outsized mincing machine and used to chop up the swedes, turnips and mangolds for the cattle. I chucked four big mangolds in him and started to turn the handle with one hand stuffing the mangolds well down with the other, and damn me if I didn't cut the top of me finger off. I goes up to Stan Russell and asked him for a bit of rag to stop the bleeding. I runs off home and my mother sent me down to the doctor, and he said you had better go to the Radcliffe Hospital. The doctor there took one look at it and then said, 'Look at that little bird up there', stuck a needle in me bum and cleaned me hand and wrapped it up. 'If you could have found the end of your finger' he said, 'I could have stuck it back on,' but it was too late for that. The parson paid £1.1.0. for the treatment, well I expect it came out of the charity money really.

Course when the buses came into service during the late 1920s we lost a lot of trade – nobody wanted to go to Oxford perched up in a carrier's cart when they could go on a nice new shiny bus, even though it cost more.

So my father and I went in to the haulage business, drawing stones (artsels) that was used for road making from the wharf, and hay and straw from farms to the railway. And when Stevens's, the baker, grocer and coal merchant in the village, had a truck of coal come in to the station, we used to unload the truck into our carts, ten tons of it, and tip it into their yard, and all for a shilling a ton.

One year my father bought a new mowing machine and went out and did contract work on the farms. Course the old men shook their heads and said that 'Them new-fangled things would be the ruination of everybody', but he proved them wrong because during the first summer the machine had already paid for itself.

Then one day we was asked to move a family from Chipping Norton to the other side of Cumnor. The man was a farm labourer. Mr Franklin, the man we was doing the job for, said 'You take my farm cart to move' um.' So on the Sunday my dad and me sets off for Chipping Norton and loads up most of the stuff that evening; course we had to sleep rough that night. Next morning we finishes loading up the beds and that, and the people – Amy Jappy and Fred Bryant and their family – and makes our way towards Eynsham. When we get to the tollgate which marks the Oxfordshire – Berkshire border, we handed 'um cart and all over to Mr Franklin who drove 'um the rest of the way to Elmwood, t'other side of Cumnor.

Then in 1917 I went to work in the garden at Stroud Court. One day old

Tony Franklin comes along and said to me, 'I've lost me whipper [that's a piece off a cart], if you can find it I'll give 'e a threep'ny bit.' So I searched till I found it and took it to him. 'Ah,' he said, 'I 'ent got a threep'ny bit at the moment, but you shall have one when I have.' Course I never did get paid for finding his whipper.

For several years I worked for a Mr Charles who kept a place called Fruitlands at the top end of the village. We grew all sorts of fruit there and one year, I think it was 1932, there was a glut of everything in the way of soft fruit, there was that much it didn't pay us to pick 'um. As it was, we had already picked twenty-five hundredweight of blackcurrants before we realized that there was no sale for them. My word we did make some homemade wine that year. Course nowadays the fruit wouldn't have been wasted. No doubt it would have gone off to the factories to be made into the famous blackcurrant drink, or put into deep freeze, and these days of 'pick your own fruit' is something that was unheard of in my younger days. Mr Charles was very particular who he had to pick his fruit, I can tell you.

After that I worked at the Oxford waterworks for several years. It was there, during our dinner times, that I saw old Ben Ayres re-enacting the mummers' play that he used to be in when he was younger. Ah, must have been thirty year now since I saw him do it. He took all the parts, that of Father Christmas, St George, the Doctor, the Turkish Knight, and the Old Woman, as best he could, doing all the actions and carrying a broom saying

> Here I come
> Little devil dout
> With my besom
> I'll sweep 'ee all out
> Money I want
> And money I'll have.

That was the Old Woman's song. Sometimes he would alter the words a bit to –

> Here comes I old Beelzebub,
> On my back I carry my tub,
> And in my hand a dripping pan
> Don't you think I'm a jolly old man.

Then he would play Father Christmas too, saying

> In comes I old Father Christmas
> Welcome in or welcome not
> Sometimes cold and sometimes hot
> I hope Father Christmas will never be forgot.

Then it would be time to start work again and we might have to wait another week before old Ben entertained us again, starting where he had left off. Perhaps on that day he would be St George fighting the imaginary Turkish Knight with his broom and injuring him, and the Doctor would be sent for and suggest a cure:

> Give him a bucket of dry hot ashes to eat
> Brush him down with a besom stick,
> And give him a yard and a half of pump water to drink.

The Doctor goes on to tell of his skills –

> I can cure the itchy pitchy
> The palsy and the gout
> Pains inside and pains without
> A broken leg or a broken arm
> Or a broken limb of any sort
> I cured old Mother Roundabout.

The last bit I remember went like this –

> Now last Christmas my father killed a fat hog,
> And my mother made black-puddings enough to choke a dog.
> And then hung them up with a pudden string,
> Till the fat dropped out and the maggots crawled in.

Mind you, I think there was a lot more to the mummers' play, but this is all that I can remember. I wish that I had learnt it all then I could have passed it on to the younger generation – as it is I don't think anybody in the village would remember any more than I have told you. Other village men that were in the mummers' play with Old Ben was Sam Molder, Bob Buck and Billy Betterton, but they have all passed on. But in their heyday they used to perform at all the big houses and pubs, collecting money as they went, just at Christmas time.

Ah, I've had many jobs in my time. I worked in Oxford in the building trade for years and years. I bought this property in 1933 for £480 – that was the house and two-and-a-half acres. There was no drains or electric when we first come here. We ran a smallholding for years, my wife doing most of the work, except for the heavy gardening. Chickens and pigs we kept too, selling the eggs, fruit and vegetables to the local people.

Now, at eighty-one, I 'ent well enough to do anything, but we jogs along, and we got some very happy memories.

~ ALICE MAY HILSDON ~
née DANCE born 1892

I was born in a small cottage in Chapel Yard, Eynsham, in the year 1892. My dad was one of the village postmen – always known as Albert Dance or Postman Dance. I went to the village school, and when I was twelve I went to Witney to sit for an examination. It was called a Labour Certificate, and if you passed it meant that you could leave school at thirteen. But I was only twelve when I left and got my first job, which was in service in a big house in Eynsham called The Gables, in Newland Street. A Colonel Gossett and his wife lived there at the time.

There were three maids and we all slept in the same bedroom right at the top of the house. It was 'up at six o'clock' every morning and we was on all day. I was the 'in-between maid'. When I was upstairs I was wanted down-stairs and when I was downstairs I was wanted up. I had lovely long hair and I always wore it down my back, but as soon as I walked into The Gables the cook said, 'You'll have to put your hair up for a start.' So I had to wear it done up in a tight bun. We wore long cotton dresses, a different one for morning and afternoon, and different aprons too. There were rows and rows of tucks round the hem of the dresses. This wasn't for decoration or fashion, but so that you could let your dresses down as you growed.

My wages was 4s. 4d. a month, and with my very first month's wages I bought my mother a half a tea service from Sawyer's shop, and it cost 2s. 9d. It was white with violets on and she thought that it was marvellous, and I was so pleased. I expect that was the first real 'set' of crockery that she'd ever had.

Oh, they give some lovely dinner parties at The Gables. Can you imagine having to wash up after a seven-course dinner, *and* coffee, for twelve people? The dirty crocks was everywhere, you didn't know where to step in the kitchen for washing up. Course they was always having people there to stay and once among the guests there was a Scotsman staying there. Well, the other maid and me was doing his bedroom, and on this particular day he'd got trousers on; we had only ever seen him in a kilt until then, he was sort of walking about the room. Then the other maid whispered to me 'Hey, his doodle's out, you'll have to tell him.' I hung back a bit 'cos we wasn't supposed to talk to the guests. Well, I was young, just about thirteen by then and still very innocent so I went up to him and said, 'Excuse me, sir, but your doodle's out.' You should have seen his face. The trouble was he had never worn a pair of trousers before in his life and he didn't realize that he had to do the buttons up.

By now our family was living in a cottage, now 71 Mill Street. So I spent my half days off at home, washing and drying my hair, it was so long I could sit on it and it was wavy too. Well, I was sitting out the front in the sun drying my hair when a man came along. He said 'What beautiful hair you have.' Course we was told not to speak to strangers so I just stared at him. He said, 'Do you live here?' I said 'Yes.' 'Are your parents in?' he asked, and I said 'Yes', and showed him round to the back of our cottage. He asked my father and mother if he could possibly take a photograph of my hair and they agreed. So I sat on an ordinary kitchen chair out in our garden with my long hair all sprayed out and hanging down over the back of the chair. This photo was to be used for an advertisement for Edward's Harlene Hair Tonic for years, and he gave me five shillings for this and it was like a fortune to me, when I thought of all them hours I worked at The Gables for 4s. 4d. a month. Then my dad asked this man if he'd got anything that was good for rubbing on a bald head to make the hair grow. So he gave my dad a free sample of Edwards pommade, yellow stuff like furniture polish it was. I think it was called Rossallene or something like that. Well, he tried it for a couple of days but it burnt his head so much he just couldn't stand it. You see the postmen's hats at that time were a sort of pillbox type and fitted very tight on the head, and of course you daren't go out without your hat in those days so we never really knew if it would have worked or not.

My dad had to deliver letters in Eynsham, Stanton Harcourt and Sutton, walking all the way of course. And sometimes folk living in the tiny hamlets couldn't get to a post office for stamps. Well, if it was a fine day they would wait outside their door till my dad come along and then they would buy a stamp off him. Other times, when he emptied the postbox it was nothing to find several pennies in there. The folk would push their letters into the post-box with no stamp on – they knew that my dad would put one on for them.

He also used to deliver medicine at the same time as he delivered the mail for Dr Cruickshank, the Eynsham doctor, and got an extra tuppence a bottle for doing this.

The first time I went on a train was on Clinch's – the Witney brewery – annual outing to Brighton. Anybody could go and it cost five shillings. I went free as I was under age. My mother wore her hat all night, she was so eager to catch that train at 5.30 in the morning. We had a lovely day, but when we was walking down a street in Brighton our mother noticed that my sister Jenny's blouse was dirty. Our mother was carrying the baby at the time. Suddenly she said 'Yer take the kid to hide yer dirty blouse.'

Well, I'd been saving my pennies for this trip, I'd put them in between the leaves of a Bible that I kept in the bottom drawer in an old wooden washstand in the bedroom. And I'd got sixpence to spend on the great day. I saw a watch in a shop window in Brighton for sixpence so went in and bought it and I cried me eyes out 'cos it had no guts in it. It was really a moneybox.   When Granny Derry died we was as pleased as punch 'cos we had a new frock each, black and white striped they was. We wished as folks had died more often, I can tell you. Mind you we always had a new frock for Whitsun, somebody in the village made them for us.

One day my sister and I hired a bike with a trailer on the back and we rode to Oxford taking it in turns to ride the bike while the other rode in the trailer. We really went to see our chaps, but told our mother that we had been to Littlemore to see our Aunt Emily. 'Well why didn't she send me some blackcurrants then?' our mother asked – you see our Auntie Emily always let us have redcurrants, blackcurrants and gooseberries. And I remember once when me and our Nance went down the Oxford Road and somebody told our mother that we was talking to some fellows, and we got a smack round the earhole when we got home.

When I was seventeen I got a job in service in a big house down the Woodstock Road in Oxford. It was a very good job too, but after a while I got fed up and give in me notice. When I told our mother that I'd give in me notice she said, 'You silly bitch you, what about me basin of dripping?' You see, the cook had a basin of dripping one fortnight and I had it the next to bring home to our mam.

One job in service that I had, in Fyfield Road, Oxford it was. But I only stayed for nine days. It was an awful place and I had to eat the food that they left. So one night I packed my few things up in my little rush basket and sneaked out, and I went to live with my future mother-in-law. She took in washing from big houses in Oxford. So I helped her until I got married.

My husband and I often used to walk from Headington to Eynsham on a Sunday to see my parents.

I can remember when Billy Morris first put the buses on the road and you had to buy a ticket *before* you could ride on the bus. The very first time I went on one was when we went to buy my daughter's pram and she will be sixty-eight come December 1981.

[61]

22 A group of children at the Infants' School, 1917 or 1918.

23 A group of girls at the Board School, 1912. Gladys Floyd, who later married Jim Evans, is the second girl from the left in the second row.

24 Preparing for a school play at the Infants' School. Gladys Floyd carries the lighted candle.

25 A Sunday School treat in the Litchfield, down the Station Road. Gladys Floyd is the tall girl on the far right; Mrs Trethewy, the girls' headmistress, is near her in the white hat.

26 Class One at Eynsham School, 1929. Far right, second row, is Jim Evans's daughter, Gladys.

27 A group of girls at the Board School. Fourth from the left, front row, is Elsie Green's sister, Nellie.

❧ ALBERT EDWARD OVENALL ☙
born 1894

Billy Williams, or 'candle fat Billy' as we kids called him, was the gas man, he carried a pole about nine feet long with a perforated cylinder on the top, with a lighted tallow candle in it so that he could light the street gas lamps, and folks swore that he never got wet because his hat and coat was so covered with tallow that had dripped from the candles that it had made them waterproof. The drag and horses used to call at The Red Lion pub with college gents from Oxford in it. They used to get the landlord to heat up a shovel full of pennies, which they provided. Then these gents would stand on top of the drag and sling the red hot pennies across the Square – and what a scramble there was too, getting one and tossing it from hand to hand and trying to stand on another while the ones in your hand cooled. But this was only successful if every kid had one – if not, there was a fight.

I remember too Gibbons brewery opposite the doctors and the ale houses – The Maltster and Shovel, The New Inn, The Fountain Inn, all gone now. Arthur Evans's father from Newland Street and Charlie Holloway from up the Abbey used to push a ten-foot-long, two-wheeled truck shaped to take five or six eighteen-gallon barrels of ale from the brewery to the pubs.

Harry Harwood, who worked for Biggers's, used to deliver the bread in a wheel-barrow covered with a flour sack. The post delivery man from Oxford came in a box van drawn by a horse, and if he only had letters he just threw them off, didn't even stop, at five o'clock in the morning too.

I was apprenticed to the bell ringing for three years. I started with Herbert Evans in 1907 and was about finished in 1910 when King Edward died. I remember helping to cap the hammers on the bell with Jason Trinder the bell master and caller, before ringing 5040 muffled changes. I think we were at it for three-and-a-half hours.

Boys employed in shops, gardens and houses were very lowly paid. I started work at eight years old. I went after school and Saturdays for fourpence a week and a penny to spend – the fourpence went to my mother.

When I was a bit older I started to help Henry Goodwin. He had a cycle business, and he used to hire out bikes to people at threepence an hour. What I had to do was help to build up cycle wheels, cutting and threading the spokes to length and fitting them to build up a wheel. For this I got three-pence, with an extra penny for 'trueing'.

I remember when the water pipes were put in the village, the navvies working shoulder-to-shoulder digging the trenches. Also being taken to the common land, leased from the council for grazing by the farmers. I was given a sickle and a fagging hook and told to cut all the thistles down. A soul-destroying job, as they seemed to grow as fast as they were cut.

A change from ordinary lessons at school was a trip to what used to be the old jail in the Square. We boys used to march down there from school for woodwork. This was the first school to be built in Eynsham – the Bartholo-mew School. It also housed the fire engine, which was often pulled by hand if no horse was available, and operated by hand of course.

Charlie Wright was an old man who lived in Acre End Street and he sold bloaters. We boys used to sing his name to the tune of 'Cherry Ripe' till he complained to Mr Trethewy our headmaster, who soon stopped that by giving the guilty boys the cane.

> Charlie Wright
> Charlie Wright
> Wright I cry
> Big fat bloaters
> Come and buy.

And once when it was election time we boys made up a song about what the government would do. We sang it to the tune of 'John Peel' and it went like this:

> They will tax us for meat
> They will tax us for bread
> And they say they will give us a pension instead.

> But the pension will come
> When we are all dead
> And the tax on the bread in the morning.

And Granny Lay used to tell me about two other tollgates, besides the one that is still used at Swinford. There was one at Barnard Gate – might be how it got its name – and one between The Elms and the Eynsham railway bridge.

Shillingford's, the wool brokers, who lived in the village at one time, used to buy up a lot of wool at shearing time. It was graded at Eynsham and then some of it was sold to the blanket mills at Witney. But most of it went 'up north' by barge through the canal system. The barges then brought back loads of coal and granite for road-making on their return journey. And once a year a load of block salt would come on the canals down to Eynsham wharf. This salt was pushed round the village on a truck and sold in blocks at sixpence each. They weighed about 20 lb and were mostly used by bakers and, of course, the breweries, because there is salt in most beers and ales, that's what makes you want another one.

Jim Wall at the rope walk often earned a penny with Bob Wall. One of them turning the wheel in a little shed at the top of Clover Place, and the other feeding the fibre. Often the rope was so long that it stretched right down the rope walk and across the road in Acre End Street. The rope was made in three, five and seven strands, depending on the thickness.

Arthur Green, the basket maker, cut his osiers in Van Dieman's land, up by The Star public house. After stripping them, he laid them in long troughs of water. Then he made baskets for the butchers and bakers and other trade folk. Granny told me about gleaning in the corn fields and taking the heads down to Cassington Mill to have them ground into flour. I have taken a basket many a time down to Johnny Juggins and collected twenty-four eggs for a shilling, duck eggs too.

At school we always celebrated Empire Day on May 24. Usually we were dressed to represent some part of the British Empire. We boys were often dressed as sportsmen from these faraway places. I remember once I was dressed as an Australian cricketer and my brother as a New Zealand All Black. In May, too the local fishermen watched for the fly to rise, and then there was a mad rush to the Evenlode, hopefully to bag a good meal.

During the wintertime we did plenty of skating and sliding – all the fields down the Cassington Road were frozen solid.

There was the famous quoits pitch in the yard of The Jolly Sportsman inn. Two three-foot square wooden frames were filled with clay, with a white feather in the centre, and steel rings, varying in weight, were tossed some forty feet to see who could score by the being nearest the feather.

One thing I shall never forget is when we had a visit, about once a year, from the dancing bears. They were big brown bears with collars on, and the man who owned them held them on a long strong chain. We were quite frightened really, but of course they couldn't get loose. The man used to chant something that sounded like this –

Na Na Na Na May   Na Na Na Na May

When he did this the bears would get up on their hind legs and jig about.

[67]

❧ DOROTHY ALDRIDGE ❧
born 1889

My parents took over The Railway Inn in 1887, coming to Eynsham from Ferry Hinksey, then from Oxford on the train. My mother told me that she carried my eldest brother Reg in her arms, walking from Ferry Hinksey to Oxford station, which would be quite two miles. I and my two sisters Glad and Marg and brother Bill were born at The Railway Inn. We were to stay there until I was nearly thirteen. It was a hard life at the pub, but our mother did have a woman who came in to do the scrubbing and washing – she was paid a shilling a day for this, but she was also given her dinner and a bottle of beer.

When I was old enough I used to help serve behind the bar – 'four ale' was tuppence a pint, and 'six ale' threepence a pint. Whisky was sold in measures, tuppence a measure, and one very prominent man in the village used to come in every Sunday morning, straight from church, and ask me to serve him with a couple of measures. Then he would dig into the pocket of his Norfolk jacket and give me a few strong white peppermints. Our mother said he bought these sweets to suck so that his breath shouldn't smell of the whisky.

We often had ostlers staying the night, taking their great stallion horses through to somewhere or other. We used to watch the men who got up very early to tend to the animals, plaiting coloured braids into their tails and manes, and brushing their coats till they shone like a polished table. The men made funny whistling noises all the time they were brushing the horses.

There were a lot of outbuildings at The Railway Inn, and we looked forward to the swallows coming every year and watched them building their nests in the stables. We never played in the streets. First of all our mother wouldn't let us, and another thing there were plenty of places to play in, lovely games we had in the stables and outhouses.

There was a big club room there where several of the village organizations met regularly, because there was no village hall at that time, you see. There was also a big room upstairs where the men played nine pins, and a bowling or skittle alley downstairs.

One of the school teachers started a children's scripture union in the clubroom and they would ask me to play the piano for the hymn-singing.

28 The Aldridge family in the yard of The Railway Inn, which they then kept. Dorothy Aldridge is holding the ivy leaves. Taken around 1900.

The teacher would announce the next hymn to be sung, and I'd say 'I'm sorry, sir, I can't play that one.' Then Mr Cobb would have to alter it to one that I did know. Mind you, I wasn't a very good piano player, but there was nobody else that could do it any better, so they had to put up with me and my very small repertoire.

Our mother was wonderful at knitting and sewing, crocheting, embroidery and tatting, and she taught us girls – Glad, Marg and me – all these things. When we were very small she made all our clothes and my brothers' too, and knitted us long vests and black stockings for wintertime. She even made my father a pair of cricketing trousers (whites) when he played for the village team. When I was ten years old I knitted my father two pairs of socks as a present and he gave me a florin for knitting them, and I thought I'd got the world.

At school, because we could sew and knit well, we girls had to knit socks during sewing lessons, for the headmaster, Mr Trethewy, and we sewed for his daughter too, making chemises and drawers – these were long, white, cotton knickers that came down to the knee. It was all chemises and drawers in those days, lace-edged and feather-stitched they were, and all women wore them.

I remember while we were at school the road was all dug up, I think it was either for the sewer or water to be laid on. Anyhow the navvies dug great deep trenches chucking up piles of thick, grey Oxfordshire clay. We used to take handfuls of this clay home and then roll it into little balls to make marbles. At night our mother would put them into the dying embers of the fire and in the morning they would be baked hard as a brick. That saved us buying marbles, you see.

In 1899 my father died, he was only forty years old too. Our mother continued to run the pub on her own, but how she managed I don't know. After about three years we left The Railway Inn – I was nearly thirteen by then – and we went to live in a cottage in another part of the village.

But that year, 1902, is the one that I remember most vividly because it was the last days of my childhood, and it was the summer particularly that I shall never forget. It was the year that the king, Edward VII, was gravely ill, and his coronation had to be put off for a while, and all the school children were so looking forward to the coronation treat that had been promised. Every Sunday prayers were said in church for the recovery of the king.

Then at last, on August 13, the coronation festivities were held in the village. Our mother had made Glad and Marg and me lovely white dresses and we had new big white hats that were very fashionable at the time, and our hair had been put in rags all night to make it nice and curly. We had white stockings and frilly petticoats and were beside ourselves with excitement.

I remember a big brass band coming to the village and the men kept playing and marching up and down the streets all day long, or so it seemed to us. Every time they passed by we all rushed to the window to wave.

At half-past two all the school children had to meet up at the Board School, then along with the teachers and the band we all paraded through the village. In the Square we stopped and sang the national anthem – it was lovely, with all the villagers joining in too. It was such a wonderful day, hot and sunny, and the cottages and houses and shops all had flags and bunting hung outside them. Then we marched back to the school and had a wonderful tea and each child was presented with a coronation mug and tuppence to spend in the Litchfield, a nice level field down the Station Road where there were roundabouts and swings and coconut shies and running races, for money too. Threepence if you came in first, tuppence second and a penny for third. I remember I won sevenpence that day and I thought I was rich, I can tell you. Glad and me went in for the three-legged race, but we got our legs tangled up and fell over, and by the time we had untangled ourselves we came in last.

There was a bicycle carnival too. Quite a number of ladies and gentlemen took part and the bikes and the riders were dressed up lovely. There were prizes for the best, but I cannot remember who won. I know that one was dressed up like a ship and another one as Britannia. When it got dark the bicycles were all lit up with their lights and lanterns hanging on them and they paraded up and down the street with the band playing and marching along in front of them.

After that we all trooped back to the Square and the crowds sang 'God Save the King,' not reverently this time, everybody seemed to be shouting with excitement, I suppose. Soon it was time to go home, but we were all so excited we couldn't go to sleep for ages. It had been a wonderful day, probably the most wonderful day of our lives, and whatever the future held in store for us, nobody could take away the memory of it.

Then I got my first job in service as under-housemaid to the Master of Pembroke College, Oxford. My wages were £8 a year. I hadn't been there long when my mother fell ill so I had to come back home to look after her. I had my hands full, I can tell you. My mother was absolutely helpless, and there were my brothers and sisters to look after as well. At the time nobody would tell me what was the matter with my mother, but I found out later that it was a very bad case of muscular rheumatism. Anyhow Dr Cruickshank said that she must wear real flannel nightgowns – of course, we always wore plain white calico ones winter and summer. Well, we had no money coming in, there was no widow's pension in those days, so how could we afford pure flannel nightgowns? The doctor must have told his wife of our plight, because before many days had gone by a parcel arrived addressed to our mother. In it were two beautiful pure flannel nightgowns. We soon got her into one of them, and from then on she started to get better. Mrs Cruikshank told me years later that she had sent to a Mr Price Jones in Wales for them, and that the money for them had come out of the church poor box.

When my mother was completely recovered the doctor asked her if she would look after a small baby which belonged to a woman who wished to go back to work. I think the doctor thought that some new interest was just what our mother needed, and that she would find the money useful as well. So she looked after the child till he was three years old. She got eight shillings a week for this – the mother found all the boy's clothes and humanized milk, whatever that was.

So I was able to go back into service again. This time I got a job at Eton in one of the college masters' houses. After two years I thought I'd move on and this was to a large mansion at Birdrop where I was paid £20 a year. It was a good place and the owners were very kind to the staff.

There was a huge room there that was called the laundry. But the laundry was sent out to be done. Roller skating was all the go and one of the maids brought a pair back with her after going home for a holiday. But the lady of the manor of Birdrop didn't really want to see her maids flying up the driveway on roller skates, so she said she could use the old laundry room. That did it – almost all the staff bought roller skates, and spent any time off down there. I didn't have any skates because I had to send most of my money home, but I used to borrow a pair from one of the other maids and got quite good at it. It was something of an achievement in those days, for a woman to be able to roller skate. What freedom too! At work we had to be so stiff and starchy in our long frocks and aprons that reached almost to our ankles and hair screwed up in a bun. But there we were, skirts and hair flying as we sped round that old laundry room, and the laughter as beginners fell down *and* showed their legs!

Then after three years I moved on again. Each time you moved in service you could usually better yourself, taking a higher job each time.

Well, I got a job at Batsford Park, Gloucestershire. There were twenty servants employed there, I was second of four housemaids and got £24 a year.

The gentry who lived at Batsford Park also had a wonderful place in Scotland. Come grouse shooting time and half the staff went up with them on the train, for two or three months. Even the laundry was sent from Scotland by train to Batsford to be done and then returned a few days later.

And all the vegetable and fruit from the garden was sent up to Scotland on the train, so was the bread and cakes which were made by the stillroom maid. We did our own bits of washing in the burn which ran through the grounds, and do you know you could smell the heather when you wore your clothes fresh clean, it was lovely. The only time we were allowed out was to church on Sundays – that was all we saw of Scotland.

That year the Great War broke out and lots of the maids lost their young men. The butler and footman went off to war as well, never to come back again. Some of the girls left and went into munitions and on the land, leaving three of us in that great house. Then part of it was taken over by the army, and the lovely gardens and grounds all went wild because there was nobody to tend them. The master and mistress did all sorts of things to help the war effort. Two of their sons were killed at Mons, only twenty and twenty-two they were, and such lovely looking men too.

During this time my youngest brother Bill contracted T.B. and he was in a pretty bad way too. Marg was at home with mother to help look after him. To help pass the time away she taught him to knit and embroider and he got quite good at it, but in the end he died, 1920 it was. Then two years afterwards Marg became ill and the doctor said that she had caught T.B. from brother Bill. So I had to give up my job and come home to help nurse her, but she died just two and a half years after Bill.

Gladys the youngest was holding down a very good job as a nursery governess, so we thought it best that she should stay there and I settled at home with mother.

Just about then Major Oakley's wife opened a handicraft shop in the village and she was looking for someone to run it. So mother and I took on the job and lived on the premises. Of course we were able to make lots of things ourselves, and Mrs Oakley took tuppence in the shilling back if we sold anything that we had made. All our spare time we knitted and crocheted, sewed and tatted.

People came for miles around to ask us to make their children's clothes, especially little girls' dresses with smocking on, which was very fashionable at the time. We did this for a number of years and people still talk about the handicraft shop and the beautiful things we made and sold there.

Then the Second World War came along and we had three young boys billeted on us. They were Londoners and not used to our country ways. But they soon settled down and stayed for three years. Never before had they worn hand-knitted socks and pullovers, or eaten boiled puddings and home-made cakes or jam. We were sorry when they went back to London:

29 Dorothy Aldridge's mother, shortly after
her marriage in 1885.

they all wrote for a little while, but I haven't heard from any of them for
thirty years or more.

   After a while mother died at the ripe old age of ninety, and then Glad
retired and came home. We put in for a council bungalow, which we got
after a little while. During the last twenty years we have both sewed and
knitted and made hundreds of things for different charities which people run
in the village. The one which both of us did most for was for Cancer Research.
But old age is creeping up fast. For the past three years Glad has been
confined to hospital and I am housebound. But at least I am still in my own
home. I have a home-help and lots of good friends, and the social workers
and doctors keep a watchful eye on me. There is so much help these days
when people are ill or infirm, then there's the pension as well. How different
from the days when my mother was left with five children to bring up and no
money coming in – just a little charity.

   But there is something missing these days – I think it is because folk have
more money and are not so dependent on their families and each other. And,
of course, a lot of the neighbourliness has gone too.

⤙ ROY BLAKE ⤚
born 1917

It was my grandfather who founded what the locals called 'Blakes' Pop Factory'. As a young man he had studied both at Cambridge and London universities, where his greatest interest had been chemistry. He came back to live first at the nearby village of Stanton Harcourt, and then finally moved to Eynsham.

When he was twenty-eight he started the business of Eynsham Mineral Waters there. In a paddock in Mill Street there is a special spring known as the 'Celebrated Spring', which is mentioned as far back as 1100. A well was sunk and the water was hand-pumped up from it for many years, and it was in this paddock that my grandfather had his pop factory built. The factory was a red-brick building and in its time it employed quite a few local people. My grandfather was convinced that the success of the mineral waters and other drinks that were produced there was because of the special properties in the water. But in 1903 everyone was put on the village water supply, which also came from a subterranean spring, so it probably made no difference to the mineral waters.

When work first started there, sometime in the late 1880s, the bottles that held the mineral waters had rounded ends, or bottoms, so that they always had to be stacked in cases – you couldn't stand them down anywhere.

Do you know, I can remember when I was a lad I saw crates of those rounded-ended bottles stacked in an old shed near the pop factory. I had to help load them onto a cart, and they were taken away and dumped some-where. If only I could remember where, I would dig them up – they would be worth a fortune now to bottle collectors.

Later, of course, came the famous 'cod' bottle, that's the one with the glass marble in. It was developed specially for holding gassy lemonade, and I was always given to understand that a vicar, 'cod' Hamilton, was the man connected with the patenting of that particular bottle. And this is how it worked. In the photograph you can see that the glass marble is resting on a ridge three parts of the way up the empty bottle. When the bottle was filled with gassy lemonade, the marble was forced to the top of the bottle, and this kept the drink airtight. When the drink was needed a special opener called

30 Lemonade and stone ginger beer bottles from Blake's lemonade factory in Mill Street. The lemonade bottles contain the glass stoppers which were so popular as marbles.

31 A crotchet-work pelmet using 'marbles' from the 'pop' factory.

a 'bottle stopper' had to be used. These special openers were fixed to the sides of bars or shop counters. The bottle top was pushed firmly against the opener, releasing the gas and sending the marble back down to the ridge.

Those glass marbles from the bottles were always very popular with the children at that time. Most of the marbles they played with in those days were either made of clay or stone. But if they could get hold of a 'stingy' or a 'tally' or a 'bottler' they were in clover. These were just a few of the local names they gave to them. Of course they had to smash the 'cod' bottle first to get them out.

You know, years ago most cottagers had a pelmet round their mantelshelf. The lovely hand-made crocheted one shown here graced one of the local villager's shelf for many years. The bobbles on it are in fact marbles from pop bottles, covered with crochet. Another use for them was to make quite an attractive necklace by covering a single marble with crochet and making a chain of the same thread. Later on the 'cod' bottles were discarded and the crown cork method was used. That was the round metal bottle top with ridges round it, and to open them you needed a small key-like opener. These were given away to the customers, so they no longer relied on the pub or shopkeeper to open their drinks bottles.

As well as mineral water, lemonade and ginger beer was produced at the factory: later on came cherry cider and other fruit drinks. The factory supplied most of the Oxford colleges as well as many hotels, pubs and shops over a wide area. In the early days, of course, all the deliveries were done with a waggon and two horses.

At one time both my father and my uncle Maurice worked with my grandfather at the factory.

My father told me a tale of how, unbeknown to his father, he once made a crafty five pounds for himself. My gramp had bought a new waggon, and a Mr Preston, who kept The Red Lion at that time, wanted to buy the old one. 'Tell him he can have it for five pounds,' my gramp said. My father goes to Mr Preston and says 'You can have the waggon, but I don't suppose you can afford to buy it.' 'How much is your father asking for it?' Mr Preston said. 'Ten pounds,' my father replied. 'Its a deal,' said Mr Preston. So my father pocketed the five pounds and handed over the other five to his father, who was quite pleased with the deal.

My grandfather used to like to do a bit of cooking in his spare time. His speciality was what he called Brasenose pastry. He had evidently got it from a chef at Brasenose College in Oxford, where apparently they used to serve it to the undergrads on special occasions.

It was a cross between a flaky and shortcrust pastry, and what a fuss and palaver it was when grandfather had a go at cooking it. He needed all the kitchen to work in. When he had mixed the pastry it was then put into a flat, greased tin, like a meat tin, and cooked in a hot oven. When it was cool he could cut it into slices about two inches wide and three inches long. On this he piled home-made strawberry jam topped with lashings of cream.

Another delicacy our family enjoyed was rook pie. We all used to go off rook shooting and then my mother, who was a farmer's daughter, made the most delicious pies you ever tasted. Not just for the family but for friends all round the county. The pies were made with just the breasts of the birds, skinned first, otherwise the meat would have tasted bitter. Well, this was layered into a dish alternately with best beef and a bit of fat bacon, seasoned well and a little liquid poured over it. Then covered with flaky pastry and cooked in a hot oven – ah, food fit for the gods it was.

My grandfather told me once about a method of charging that some of the tradesmen of that time used, whereby they diddled the customers out of a few pence. For some reason it was called the 'Lipton' method and this is how it worked. Say three items were added up – threepence ($3d.$), ninepence halfpenny ($9\frac{1}{2}d.$) and fourpence halfpenny ($4\frac{1}{2}d.$). The tradesman would say, very quickly, 'Let me see: that's seventeen pence, that'll be $1s.$ $7d.$ please' – making tuppence – and thirty-six pence became $3s.$ $6d.$, forty-eight pence $4s.$ $8d.$, and so it went on. That few pence profit, or should I say diddling, doesn't sound much these days, but do that to several customers over a period of time and you make a fair bit. Of course, some of the poor old folk were not too bright and they were the poor devils that were diddled out of a few coppers that meant so much to them.

I used to help out at the factory during my school holidays, and I can remember sitting on a stool with a great big red earthenware pan in front of me that was filled with ginger beer. My job was to bottle the stuff off into creamy coloured, half-pint stone bottles, but first I had to pour the liquid through a big gauze funnel. My grandfather mixed his own ingredients to make the ginger beer, and the essences for the other drinks were very carefully measured out by him too.

Some of the bottles containing the drinks had the wording printed on them in black lettering, but those that didn't had to have sticky labels put on them, all by hand too, and that was another job I had to do during my holidays.

But during the 1930s the trade went down considerably. A firm called White's came into the trade and were offering a *twenty-ounce bottle* of lemonade for a penny, while Blake's were charging a penny for a ten-ounce one.

Around this time too my uncle Maurice fell out with my grandfather and left to start his own lemonade factory in the village up the Witney Road. Of course he had all new machinery there and really did very well. My father was keen to get back into working as a mechanic with cars and lorries so in time the original pop factory in Mill Street folded up.

My uncle Maurice continued to run his factory up until 1961 when he retired. Another firm rented the factory, still producing drinks, for a couple of years, but they didn't seem to do very well. After letting it to yet another drinks firm for a while, the place was finally let to a garage owner and this year [1980] the building was actually sold.

The old original red-brick pop factory in Mill Street remained empty all through the years, save for part of it being used as a garage and workshop by its present owner, a Mr Harris.

But it had one brief moment of glory. During a drought Eynsham's own spring that served the whole village had all but dried up, and the locals went with buckets and bowles to the paddock in Mill Street, and John Harris and his brother Mervyn stood for hours pumping up water from the 'Celebrated Spring'.

32 The Railway Inn in 1907 – the year after Dorothy Aldridge's family left.

IVY HANKS

née PERRIN *born* 1913

I started work at Blake's mineral factory in Mill Street when I was about seventeen and I earned ten shillings a week.

We youngsters did all sorts of jobs. One of these was washing the 'marble' bottles when they came back from the customers. Mr Blake was very particular about this, and we had to scrub the outsides of the bottles with small scrubbing burshes, in cold water too. But the insides of the bottles were washed by a little contraption which was fixed on to the end of a tank of water. There were twenty-four little pipes with nozzles on the end of them. We shoved the bottles on to the end of the nozzles, then with a hand-pump we pumped up a spray of water, and it was this spray that washed the insides of the bottles. All the water that was used in the factory came from the special spring, but all of it had to be hand-pumped up.

Bottles with paper labels on were soaked in the tank of water so that the old label came off easily.

During the bottling of the gassy lemonade quite a few of the 'marble' bottles got broken. One I remember exploded in the face of one of Mr Blake's sons, Phillip it was, and he had that scar under his chin all his life.

We used to chuck the broken or faulty bottles into a heap in the corner of the factory, and some of the villagers would come with their wheelbarrows and cart them away. They used them to make edgings round their gardens, turning the bottles upside-down and thrusting the neck part into the soil. Sometimes little ferns grew up in the bottles and they looked quite pretty. Other broken bottles we would load up onto the cart, and Bob Buckingham took them down the Station Road somewhere and dumped them in an old gravel pit.

Blake's Ginger Beer was another speciality made there. Mr Blake always mixed this brew up himself. He had two big red earthenware pans and two huge wooded tubs in which he used to mix it, using root ginger, cream of tartar, yeast and essences – and water, of course. The containers were then covered with thick cloths for about three days, while it was fermenting. Then it was strained and bottled off into screw-topped half-pint stone bottles. Oh yes, Blake's Ginger Beer was a very popular drink in those days.

But in the early 'thirties the pop factory in Mill Street closed when one of Mr Blake's sons went into the garage business and the other, Maurice, opened his own lemonade factory in the village, a new building up the Witney Road. I worked there till I got married. Then a few years afterwards the Second World War broke out and the men had to go off into the forces, and Mr Blake asked me to go back to work. I did, driving the lorry mostly, delivering soft fruit drinks all round the countryside. It was heavy work lifting those crates of full bottles, but I got used to it and quite enjoyed it. I even stayed on after the war. Then Mr Blake retired, so did I soon after. And his factory has since been used for all sorts of things.

33 The site of Blake's 'pop' factory, by the 'Celebrated Spring'.

❧ TEMPERANCE BEATRICE HAWTIN ❧
née HANKS *born* 1904

We was all born up High Street, next to Biggers's the bakers. There was seven of us in the family and my father was a hurdle-maker – what you'd call self-employed.

The first thing I can recall is that when I was about three year-old, one of my cousins had come over from Oxford and he had brought little presents for the Christmas stockings – well, so I learned in later years. My brother was sitting in the kitchen pulling on his boots and I stood by the fire watching him, when my nightdress caught fire and I was badly burnt. But the neighbours were ever so good and always popping in with little treats for me, and 'Auntie Kate' – no relation, but a wonderful neighbour – brought me a lovely milky rice pudding and a fluffy Yorkshire pudding every Monday until I got better. Neighbours were like that in them days.

And on the day when one of my brothers was 'britched', that's what they called it when little boys, who in them days wore frocks and petticoats till they was nearly five, wore their first pair of trousers, blue velvet they was what our mother had made for him, well on this special day, 'Tailor' Harris, Auntie Kate's husband, put a penny in my brother's trouser pocket and he thought he was in heaven. As a matter of fact, my mother made all my brothers' suits, even when they was growed up – the first 'boughten' suit one of them had was when he went into the army during the First World War.

The village was a lovely place when we was children and growing up. All the tradesmen called round the cottages and houses with their goods.

The baker called every day, coming indoors with his big wicker basket slung over his arm. The basket was filled with new, hot, crusty loaves that smelt beautiful. He used to let me scrump up some of the crumbs that lay in the bottom of the basket. I'd wet me finger with my tongue and dip me finger in. I used to collect quite a lot of crumbs that way, Oh they was lovely too. Another daily caller was the milkman, old Jesse Treadwell, but everybody pronounced it 'Treadle'. He worked for Franklin's, the big dairy farmers at Swinford, about a mile out of the village, and Jesse used to have to push a two-wheeled milk handcart, with a big churn on it that held ten or twelve gallons of milk, up to the village. And when it was slippery and frosty he couldn't manage to get the heavy cart up the slope on his own. So he would recruit the first two schoolboys that he could get hold of to help him. Rope would be fixed on to the cart and the lads went in front pulling like a couple of young colts. The big churn on the cart had a tap fixed on it, and from this Jesse refilled his two-gallon can again and again, and this was the one he carried round to the houses. Inside the can, hanging just at the top, was a little ridge where he hung his pint and half-pint measures. They was steel too and almost cup-shaped, with handles. He would dip them down into the big can and bring out lovely fresh milk. Our mother always kept a quart jug ready for him to tip it into. Mind you, some poor folks hadn't got a jug – then old Jesse would have to pour the milk into a basin or bowl. But wet or fine, snow or hail, the tradesmen never let you down. And they was always cheerful, joking and laughing about with the housewives, bringing them bits of news and gossip, and whistling and singing as they went about their work.

Other tradesmen called: there was a Mr Pitts who cycled five or six miles from Woodstock once a week to sell us fish, and a Mr Buckingham, a jeweller and clock-mender, he too came from Woodstock on a bike. Whereas Mr Pitt came once a week, Mr Buckingham only called fortnightly. I don't suppose he sold much jewellery in our village, but no doubt he found a few clocks and watches to mend. He also sold wedding rings with a present given for every purchase, and reading spectacles at a shilling a time. There was Mr Wright who pushed a truck about the place selling odds and ends – we used to holler after him, 'Mr Wright, you're not quite right,' and then run away as fast as we could in case he caught us.

Then there was the rag and bone man. He had a little truck too that he pushed about and he would give us a penny for a rabbit skin, you could hear him all over the village calling, 'Any rags bones or rabbit skins.' Of course as the years went by Mr Pitts and Mr Buckingham and the rag man all had a pony and trap or a cart, but when we was small children they didn't.

We often had travelling gypsies come round selling clothes pegs and bits of odds and ends. One woman, a Mrs Pratley, came round regular, she'd call at our house and ask 'Anything out the basket, lady?' There were knots of tape and elastic, bootlaces and clothes pegs that her husband used to make from willow sticks, and soap, two sorts: she'd say to our mother, 'Now ma'am, do you want scented or disinfection?'

We was well catered for in every way. There were five bakers and that many grocers' shops. Pimm's and Sawyer's sold household goods and boots and shoes, tools and bikes. We had a very good chemist besides two barbers and shoe menders and a basket-maker, and, for them as wanted 'um, thirteen pubs. Oh yes, this was a very busy little place when we was all young.

I remember Tom Hall, one of our village bakers, telling our mother what a job he had to get in some of the money that was owed for bread from some of the folks hereabouts. Often poor people would give him a couple of homemade rugs in lieu of payment for bread! 'I don't want thur blummen rag rugs,' he told her, 'but if I didn't accept them I shouldn't have anything.'

Then there was an old man who used to call about twice a year to see if we had any scissors or knives that wanted sharpening. Old Ned was the only name that he was known by. He was a small man with a beard and he had some sort of contraption fixed on to his bicycle. I know that there was a sharpening stone on the bar of his bike. He would stand the bike on a stand, then pedal round and round – this sent the sharpening stone round. He would lay the knife edge lightly on the stone, it made a tinkling sound, and when he'd finished the blade was razor sharp. I think he came from somewhere in the Midlands and he made his living by working his way up and down the country searching for customers.

Our mother always had what she called 'me dress-making scissors' sharpened by him, but our dad always saw to the ordinary knives and things. He had what most folks owned and that was a whetstone, a bluey grey sharpening stone which was bought from the ironmongers, and he kept his sickle and scythe sharpened up on it too.

Course people was either strong church or chapel in them days. We was chapel and every Sunday a Mr and Mrs Wallace and Mr R. E. Alden and Grace Alden used to come from Oxford to Eynsham and they used to preach all day, or so it seemed to us. Mind you, they was very good to the poor folk in the village, and Mr Harris the carrier used to bring parcels of free meat from Alden's the butchers on Saturday nights. There was lots of poor folks waiting for the carrier's cart to draw up in the Square. We used to get extra meat because we let the Aldens leave their horse and brougham in our yard all day every Sunday. And when they came to collect the horse and brougham on Sunday night they would often come into our kitchen, and our mother would fetch out some cold rabbit pie and they would eat it up as sweet as a nut. Mind you, there was a woman in the village who used to get the fancy lace-edged tablecloth out and her best silver and give them a bit of tea, but they was still very glad of our mam's cold rabbit pie.

We got most of our rabbits from Watts the farmers. We ate a lot of rabbits, and we had plenty of suet puddings too – currant (spotted dick as we called it), jam rolypoly, and meat puddings galore.

I never liked school very much, but if you went every day of the week the teacher would let you go home early on a Friday.

When I was thirteen I worked for a Mrs Preston down Swan Lane, for about an hour before school and an hour after. I done rough housework, scrubbing and that, all for sixpence a week. And while I was there Mrs Preston gave me a book of the parish magazines for 1903 to 1904, because my christening was reported in there. The parish magazine in them days was quite thick: it came out each month and it had stories and household hints as well as the births, marriages and deaths, and all the village activities. All the local tradesmen advertised in it. Mine was a whole year's magazine made into a thick book. I've got it now and it just shows how things have altered since then. And I still got a fourpenny piece that I found in a piece of Christmas pudding that Mrs Preston gave me once.

During the First World War my sister Daisy was trained at Drayton St Leonard's to be a farm worker: our mother too did farm work at that time. All Daisy took with her when she was ploughing was a bottle of cold tea. And as soon as I was old enough I went and did farm work. After thirty days you earned yourself an army armlet, green they were with a crown on. Princess Mary presented me with mine, somewhere in Oxford it was, and I was one of the youngest there to receive this award.

Course the work was all so different then. Do you know, a horse used to walk round and round attached to an iron bar all day in a circle to work an elevator which carried the hay up to make ricks in the fields and farmyards – poor devils, we used to call 'um monkeys. And my sisters Daisy and Ada used to give us tuppence a week for going without sugar, so that our mother could have it to make jam with.

We children would go anywhere in the village if we knowed that somebody was killing a pig. The old pig killer used to throw the pigs' toenails to us and we used to suck them – they was lovely, and didn't we get our faces black too! The pigs was burnt after they had been killed – well the bristles were burnt off 'um with lighted straw – I don't know who was blackest, we or the pig. During the war the government billeted three soldiers on us. They had to sleep in the attic and the slates was all loose and a lot of them missing. So the landlord had to put a few slates on or otherwise that would have rained in on them soldiers. A horse-drawn waggon used to bring their rations every Friday, I think the waggon belonged to a man called Harold Honour.

Then we had the chance of a better house in the High Street, well that part called Acre End Street now, and do you know the soldiers moved our bits of furniture on an army cart.

That was a dreadful war the 1914–18 one. My brother went into the army

[85]

and he got malaria ever so bad and was sent home on leave. We girls set off down to the station to meet him. But we never saw him. We was walking back home crying when the vicar met us and asked us what was wrong. We told him our brother was supposed to be coming home. So he said he'd gone home, he had altered so much and looked so ill we hadn't recognised him.

One day our mother went to Pimm's shop to buy a pair of boots for my younger brother Reg, who was just five years old. They was hobnailed boots too and they cost half-a-crown and they was that heavy you could hear him coming right up the top end of the village, clattering along on the stony road.

To earn a few coppers our mother used to do sewing for a family who lived near us. One day the woman asked her to make a pair of trousers for one of her young sons. It wasn't new material, either; first our mother had to unpick a pair that had belonged to the boy's father, that had worn out at the knees. Anyhow she made the trousers, lined them with calico, put five buttons and buttonholes up the flies and buttons all round for the braces. She had been charging sixpence for this sort of sewing, but she asked me to tell the woman that they had gone up to eightpence. The woman was flabbergasted and said, 'Go back and ask your mother if she has made a mistake.' I went out to the yard and stood there a few minutes, pretending to go home, then went back to the woman and said, 'Yes, she has made a mistake, it should be a shilling.' She gave me the shilling very grudgingly, and I went home and told my mother what had happened. She grumbled at me and said that the woman probably wouldn't give her any more work, but she did, she knew when she was well off.

We children always went to the Baptist chapel on Sunday mornings, Sunday school in the afternoon and chapel again at night. And always before we went at nights in the wintertime our mother would give us each a cup of hot gravy.

One Sunday afternoon I was going to Sunday school and I had just turned the corner of Lombard Street when I saw a sight that made me bust out laughing. Two men had got another man, who was very drunk, in a wheelbarrow and they was trying to push him home. I daren't tell you their names 'cos their relations wouldn't like it. Well, as I said, they was trying to push this man home, and they was in a tidy state themselves. Well, they got the wheel stuck down the cellar grating (that grating is still there to this day), and the two men was a hollering and shouting at one another to push harder when ass over head goes the lot, three men and a wheelbarrow went rolling into the road. Lord knows how they got on after that. I just squittered up the path to the chapel as fast as I could, still laughing fit to bust.

[86]

WINIFRED MAY ELLIS
née HIRONS *born* 1901

AND

IDA JANE HEPENSTALL
née HIRONS *born* 1898

There was fourteen of us in our family, and we were all born in Newland Street, Eynsham, where our father kept a butcher's shop which had been handed down to him from his father. We were lucky: our house was quite big and we had a pony and trap, and a horse and cart for delivery, which was in Eynsham and Cassington mostly. Our mother made lovely faggots, and everybody said how wonderful tasty they were. Our elder brothers used to take them round the village and sell them, hot. They also took them round to the surrounding villages too, Northleigh, Hanborough, Yarnton and Cassington, mostly on Saturday nights. They only cost a penny each, and people still talk about the wonderful flavour even to this day.

We girls used to help our mother clean the pigs chitterlings. Our arms used to ache till we thought they'd drop off, as we held up jug after jug of cold water to pour down through the pigs' innards to clean them. She used to cook these too to be sold in the shop.

Course we all went to the village school. I [Winifred] only got the cane once, but can't remember what I had it for. And we were never allowed to play in the streets. Anyhow there was that many in our family we never needed anybody else to play with. In the wintertime we used to play in the greenhouses, our dad had two or three very big ones in our garden. He used to grow lots and lots of tomatoes which were sold in the shop. And he grew the most beautiful grapes, he had his special customers for these. The secret of growing such wonderful crops of both tomatoes and grapes was the fact that the blood from the slaughterhouse, which was just at the back of the shop, was fed to them. We sold hundredweights of tomatoes every year. The garden was very big and grew enough fruit and vegetables for all our big family. Do you know, not one of us ever had to have the doctor while we lived at home, and our mother made everything, all our clothes, for the boys as well as we girls, and of course she made lots of jam, puddings and wines. She used to make hop bitter, too. Our mother was always working, from

[87]

dawn till dusk, either in the house or in the garden. Of course as soon as they were able our brothers helped in the butcher's shop. Our dad was het up with rheumatics all his life, he reckoned it was working in the slaughterhouse when he was a lad, sloshing water about to swill the place down. He always walked with a limp as far as I can remember. Do you know, we used to have five bakers call with bread every day – that was Biggers's, Cox's, Whitlock's, Hall's and Stevens's. These were bakers who had businesses in the village at that time. And sometimes one from Hanborough used to deliver bread as well. The idea of having all of them call was so that all of them in turn would buy their meat from us. Course there was no motor cars about in them days, everything was delivered by horse and cart or push cart. In his day our gramp even served Blenheim Palace with meat, and he used to breed pups for them. They were spaniels and each had to have a white spot in the middle of its forehead. Our father even went shooting once with King Edward VII. That was what the dogs were used for that our gramp reared, for the big shooting parties that they used to have at Blenheim. Once there were two of the puppies that our gramp called rejects, just because the markings on them weren't quite perfect, so we had them as pets and called them Queenie and Daisy.

At Christmas time there was dozens of braces of pheasants hung up in our shop – these, of course, came from the Blenheim estate. I suppose all the gentry around bought them, and there was some gentry about then I can tell you. The poor working people could never afford to buy pheasants at that time; they were lucky if they had a rabbit or two or a cockerel what they had reared themselves in their back gardens.

I remember one day when I was in the shop a poor woman from our street came and said to our dad, 'I wants a pig's head, Mr Hirons, cut as near to his ass as possible.' People was like that in those days, make a joke out of nothing they would.

When our father had bought live pigs and sheep and cattle at the market or from farmers, and he wasn't ready to kill them, they would be kept in a field down the Oxford road opposite Johnny Juggins. When they were needed they would drive them up to the slaughterhouse at the back of the shop to kill them. Once I remember we was all quite frightened when a cow smashed through the railings and tried to get out.

We had to go to church on Sundays, but in the evenings our father would read to us and teach us all sorts of things. Our sister is ninety and can still recite a poem he taught her. And we can all still say the alphabet backwards even at our age. He had a lot of patience with us children.

But our mother used to work so hard, and she died when she was forty and there were still five of us at school. We sisters were both good at sewing and used to make the teachers' underclothes, all by hand of course, during the sewing lessons. And some of our needlework was exhibited at the Town Hall at Oxford. We both left school at thirteen. One of us went as an apprentice dressmaker to a Mrs Harvey in Oxford, and the other one in service.

Then a sad thing happened. Next to our house and the shop and slaughterhouse was a big house called Newland House, and a new man came along and bought it. He wanted to make his garden bigger and he didn't want a butcher's next door, so he bought the property from our father and our lovely big house and shop was pulled down. That was over sixty-six years ago. And until a new estate went up in 1962 there, in one part of the grounds of Newland House, you could still see remains of our slaughterhouse and pig sties and the dog pens.

When the Great War came along, one of us got a job making bell tents and the other went into munitions at Woolwich Arsenal. Life was never quite the same after that war of 1914–18.

34 A view of Newland Street, taken by Mr Howe, the chemist and postmaster.

❧ IDA MABEL ANNE HOPKINS ❧
born 1893

My father had a farm at Pinkhill, Eynsham, where I and my youngest sister were born. I had two older sisters who were born at a farm near Freeland, about three miles away from the village. Pinkhill, or Puncle as it was pronounced by the locals, was a lovely farm bordering the river Thames. My father also ran Salutation Farm, just along the Witney Road from Eynsham. Our parents were very strict, but we were a very happy family.

At first we girls all went to the Infants' School in the village, in Swann Street. We were taken there by pony and trap because the farm was some way out of the village. Quite often in the wintertime the river would flood and cover the meadows for a time, and it would come right up and into the walled garden, flooding the two ends of the house, the dairy at one end and the scullery at the other, but the water never came into the farmhouse living quarters. During these flooding periods we used to have to be taken to school part of the way in a boat.

When we got older we went to the Methodist school in the nearby town of Witney. By now my eldest sister was old enough to drive the pony and trap so we made the trip to school every day that way. Later on I went to the grammar school at Witney. I was always interested in country and morris dancing, and played hockey and tennis, not just at school but for many many years afterwards. While I was at Witney Grammar School I had four years' tuition on the organ in St Mary's Church which was nearby. And for several years I played the organ at the Methodist chapel services in Eynsham.

My father was very fond of children, and whenever he saw some in the village he would stop and pick them up in his pony and trap and give them a ride round and a few sweets. Course that was quite a little treat for the poorer children.

He was a very good cricketer too and played for the village side. I remember that Mr Trethewy, the schoolmaster, used to play about the same time, and although my father couldn't swim, he once saved a man who was trying to drown himself in the Thames at Pinkhill.

My father kept a breed of very long-horned cattle. I don't remember what sort they were but you don't ever see any about these days like them. He used to travel to Worcester and to Devonshire to purchase his cattle, and often won prizes at the market for his bulls.

One thing that always remains very vivid in my mind is the harvest times and the lovely picnics we children had in the fields. Women used to come from Stanton Harcourt to do farm work at harvest time. They wore white bonnets and long white aprons and blue cotton frocks, and they used big wooden rakes, working in a line across the haymaking fields. My father was the first farmer in the area to have a hay pitcher to toss the hay on the carts instead of the workmen having to pitch it up by hand with hay forks.

The same women who helped on the farm also used to help in the house too. We had our own bakehouse where we baked all our bread and cakes. And of course there was always plenty of washing to do with four growing girls and our parents. Our farm lay midway between Eynsham and Stanton Harcourt and the women used to walk along a right of way from their village to Pinkhill.

When I was a young girl the Boys' Brigade from Witney used to come for a week's camp to our farm during the summer holidays. Mr Harold Early, head of the famous Witney Blanket Mills, was in charge of the boys, and always on their last night they would entertain us with a singsong in the barn.

I remember when we could just go down the field from the farm and across a bridge and walk to Cumnor meadow and then on to Oxford. And one year I stood in that first field on a lovely spring day, knee deep in cowslips. I have never seen so many as there were that year, simply smothered with them the grass was, and the delicate scent that rose from them as I walked is something that I shall never forget.

We were a very musical family, we all played some instrument or another, some of us more than one. I started to learn to play the piano when I was five years old. We had wonderful Sunday night singsongs round the piano, after we had all been to chapel.

After I left the grammar school I went on to the Western School at Headington. I had to stay in lodgings for five days, just coming home at the weekends. I stayed there until I was twenty-four. Then I was offered a place at Brize Norton village school – I took it and stayed there until I retired. One year I remember we had terribly deep snow, so deep that the buses couldn't run. So one day I got up early and struggled down to Eynsham station and caught the seven o'clock train and I arrived at Brize Norton school, about 6 miles away, at midday. Another day during a snowstorm the bus that I was travelling in ran into a ditch and we were stranded for hours.

In 1931 my father retired from farming and he had a house built in the village, where I still live. Within fifteen months my mother had died, and three months after that my father passed away too. My elder sisters had left to be married so there was just me and my younger sister left. She too fell ill and died ten years after coming to live here.

For thirty years I ran the women's meeting at the Eynsham Methodist chapel; now it is closed, but we still hold our weekly meetings, in the vicarage now. For many years I have belonged to the Women's Institute, and have played the piano for the W.I. drama, pantomimes and other dramatic activities. During the past ten years I've taken up painting as a hobby, and I enjoy this very much. Our tutor, Miss L. Buchanan, painted my portrait, and in 1978 it was chosen to be hung in the Royal Academy in London.

I am very crippled now and attend hospital for treatment, but I still take an interest in many things, local history, painting, W.I. and of course my women's meeting. I have lots of visitors and kind people who help me.

35 The bridge by The Talbot Inn.

❧ ELSIE MAY GREEN ☙
née JEFFERIES *born* 1902

We were ten in family. Mind you five of them died when they were very young – well they did in them days, didn't they? My father was a shoemender and I've known him sole and heel a pair of boots for the top of a loaf, we was that hard up.

He blew the organ at the church on Sunday mornings and then it was down to The Queen's Head pub afterwards for a drink and to get a bit of 'snobbing' trade. And he would often bring a few pairs of boots back to mend. And as soon as he'd had his bit of Sunday dinner, it was out with the leather and his iron foot and a mouth full of boot nails, and he would get on with boot-mending so as he could take them back on Monday morning and get a few shillings for mam.

Do you know, he used to walk into Oxford to buy his leather, and then stop at Johnny Juggins at The Talbot on the way back for a drink? I suppose he reckoned he had earned a half pint after walking to Oxford and back.

Sometimes folk would give him their very old boots and shoes and he would alter them so that they fitted us kids. Course they was most uncomfortable, no wonder I got bunions as big as ducks' eggs.

One day my dad climbed a tall walnut tree to pick some nuts, he fell out the tree and broke his leg. He died of T.B. when he was fifty, but falling out of that tree hastened his death – well, that's what the doctor told mam.

My mam was left a widow with five children, and the youngest was only six months old. Course there was no pension. All the help we had was two-and-sixpence and two large loaves a week from the charities. I used to have to go each week to Mr Stansfield, the relieving officer, who lived in Newland Street, to ask for that half a crown. Talk about feeling like a beggar. Then it was down to Biggers's bakehouse to ask for the two loaves of bread. They used to book it down and then claim off the charities for the cost.

My mother went out charring for sixpence an hour – washing, scrubbing and general cleaning. My two eldest brothers did work before and after school. One worked at the mineral works in Mill Street – we kids called it the 'pop factory' – and the other at Franklin's farm at Swinford, just beyond

[93]

Eynsham toll bridge. But as soon as they were old enough they were called up for the army, one in the Engineers and the other in the Field Artillery. The one in the Artillery was wounded in the battle of Mons and had some shrapnel in his head all his life, but it didn't seem to bother him and he lived until he was eighty-four.

I went to work for Mrs Arthur Blake before school to get the wood and coal in and do the grates, then again in the evening to do the washing up, and I got 2s. 6d. a week for this. Mam did their weekly washing, and the night before it was my job to fill up the copper with water and then pop round early the next morning and light the fire underneath it, so that the water was hot enough for her to start as soon as we had gone to school. And because Mam was often out doing washing and housework, I had to take my youngest sister up to the Board School with me because there was nobody at home to look after her and she was too young to go to the Infants' School.

Then mam began to get laundry from some of the Oxford college gents. It was brought dirty and took back clean by Mr Batt's carrier's cart. I can remember some of the prices which were very poor. All she got was 3d. for washing, drying and ironing a shirt.

When I left school I went to work for a Mrs Clayton who kept a lodging house for Land Army girls, it was that big house in Thames Street opposite Pimm's shop. There was a lot of outbuildings where the horses and carts and machinery was kept. While I was there I had a terrible bad throat and she told my mother that I ought to have a doctor. Mind you, nobody went to the doctors if they could help it because you had to pay. Anyhow I got that bad so Mam took me along. That was in 1916, and the doctor said that I had got diphtheria and said that I had most likely caught it off the horses. I was sent off to Abingdon isolation hospital. After I got better the matron asked me if I'd go and work there as ward maid, so I said yes. I was to get £18 a year, and I had to send mam ten shillings a month. I got a day off once a month too and used to come home on the train.

Then there was that terrible 'flu epidemic during the First World War and I got it, and it turned to pneumonia. They sent for mam and she stopped the night I was that bad. I'd only just got over that when I went down with scarlet fever, so it was off to the isolation ward again.

Well, after that I came back to Eynsham and got a job at Franklin's at Swinford, just outside the village. I was employed as housemaid and slept in. The housekeeper was a miserable old thing too. I got £18 a year and all found, and that meant that beside the food, the mistress also provided my morning and afternoon dresses, caps and aprons. But I only stayed a year there. You see one Sunday, late afternoon it was, I was rushing about getting the tea ready for the missus. And the reason I was rushing was because I wanted to go up the village to chapel. Well, in my haste I fell down with the tray and broke two of her best china cups and saucers, and the old devil stopped the cost of them out of my wages. So that was it, I up and left. My next job was at a Mrs Hubbard's at The Orchard in Queen Street, only a stone's throw from home. I stayed there for years, they were ever such nice people and they owned the Belfast Linen Shop in the High Street in Oxford. While I was there I had a big hard lump come up on my wrist and this Mrs Hubbard paid £2 so that I could have it removed. But it was never done because it was too near Christmas and I couldn't be spared to go to hospital to have it done. And I've still got that lump on my wrist. I often wonder who it was had that £2 of the missus's for nothing.

Mam also worked on the land during the war. She wasn't in the Land Army like some of the women in the village, but she did wear a special armband, a sort of auxiliary I suppose you would call her. She did all sorts of work, threshing and feeding the cattle, and once she was driving a horse and cart and the darn thing run away with her. I've seen her come home from a day's work on the farm in wintertime with her skirts frozen round her legs.

Years later she had to have one of her legs off and she told me that it all started from when she knocked it badly on our old iron bedstead. I suppose she was so busy working to try and keep us kids that she didn't take care of herself. Well, the hospital fixed her up with an artificial leg but she could never get on with it. But she managed to get about the house and yard (and still take in washing) by using an old kitchen chair, sort of lodging the stump on it, and walking it along as it were.

I remember as a child I was often sent down to Biggers's for three pen'orth of coal that I used to fetch in an old pram, and a pen'orth of sugar, we was that hard up – God above we was hard up, I can tell you! But Mam always tried to make it nice at Christmas for us. We'd hang up a stocking or sock and she always managed to put a bit of something in each. Usually there was an orange and apple, and for us girls a little row of beads, a screw of dolly mixtures and a cheap little doll. The boys would have a pop gun and a few marbles. All this stuff was bought from Pimm's shop in the square. Mind you we always had a special treat from an old aunt who lived at Aston a few miles away. She sent us a nice box of fruit regular every Christmas.

There wasn't a lot of chance to play – if we wasn't looking after younger brothers or sister, we was off down the lanes wooding, pram loads of wood I've got in my time. And in the autumn we used to go blackberrying and sell them to Cooper's of Oxford – you know, the famous marmalade makers. Well, they was on some sort of contract to make jam for the troops. Lots and lots of folks round here went blackberrying to earn a few coppers. We loved it when our brothers came with us. You see there was lots of blackberries as we couldn't reach – always the biggest and best seemed to be in the middle of a great bush or high up in the hedge. Well, the boys would find a hurdle, perhaps one that was stopping up a gap in the hedge, then they would fling the hurdle across a great bush and use it as a sort of ladder; that way they could reach the blackberries in the middle. We used to get halfpenny a pound for 'um. We took them into Oxford – walking, pushing them in an old pram, then took it in turns to have a ride home. Ah, that was a good ten miles there and back.

Well, Mam worked hard all her life and so did I. When my boys was tiny I went out scrubbing and cleaning, pushing them in the pram wherever I was working. They'd sit there while I got on with it. For years and years I worked at The Swan Inn in the village, cleaning mostly.

Well, in time my family of three boys got married with homes of their own and my husband George and me got the pension. We was better off than we'd ever been when he was working as a builder's labourer. And just as we thought we was going to sit back and take it easy for a few years, a tragedy happened in the family. My youngest son's wife died of cancer. She was ever such a nice girl too and so kind to me. They had two young boys, one three years old, the other just a year. So I said I'd have them, and my youngest sister who lives very near to us said that she would help me with them. I should never have been able to manage the lads without her, after all I was over seventy. She bathed them and did the washing and helped with the cooking and took them out for walks, and often had them round at her house to give me a break. Now they are both at school, and because I haven't been well this year, I only have the boys for 'bed and breakfast' and my sister has them for the rest of the time, taking and fetching them from school and all that. Of course my youngest son lives with me, so at least the boys have got their dad with them. And whatever happens in the future my sister and I feel that we have helped the grandchildren over the worst time in their young lives.

36 Mr Floyd, photographed in about 1880.

37 The man paying to go through the toll-gate is Jim Evans's father-in-law, John Floyd; taken around 1900.

38 The Swinford toll bridge.

39 The toll bridge in the early 1900s with Beacon Hill in the background.

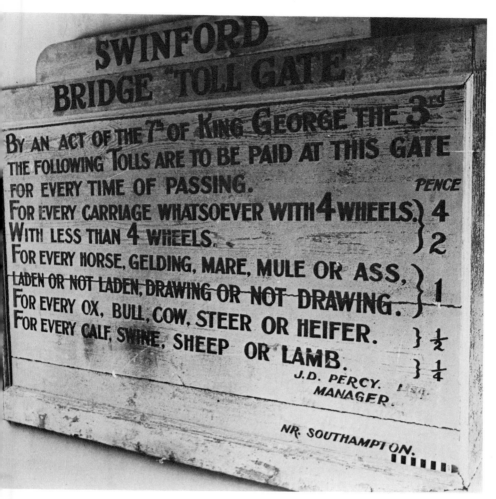

SWINFORD
BRIDGE TOLL GATE

BY AN ACT OF THE 7ᵗ OF KING GEORGE THE 3ʳᵈ
THE FOLLOWING TOLLS ARE TO BE PAID AT THIS GATE
FOR EVERY TIME OF PASSING.

	PENCE
FOR EVERY CARRIAGE WHATSOEVER WITH 4 WHEELS.	4
WITH LESS THAN 4 WHEELS.	2
FOR EVERY HORSE, GELDING, MARE, MULE OR ASS, LADEN OR NOT LADEN, DRAWING OR NOT DRAWING.	1
FOR EVERY OX, BULL, COW, STEER OR HEIFER.	½
FOR EVERY CALF, SWINE, SHEEP OR LAMB.	¼

J.D. PERCY.
MANAGER.

NR. SOUTHAMPTON.

40 The old board which used to hang on the wall at Swinford toll-gate, and is now in the Woodstock museum.

⊸ DAISY PRATLEY ⊱
née DRUCE

I was born in Eynsham in that big house, Llandaff, in the Square. There were ten of us in family and my father was quite a big farmer. But when I was six years old my mother died and some of us children were sent away to a boarding school for many years.

Then I came back home to keep house for my father, who by then had moved to Newland Street. Later we were to move to my present home to this cottage in High Street. The rent was two shillings a week when we first came here, over fifty years ago.

Old Joey Pimm used to live here before us – he was the local barber, and cut men's hair for tuppence and boys for a penny.

I remember when we first came here the living room ceiling was made of canvas and mortar, and the floor was covered with big stone slabs.

With my brothers and father to look after I didn't have much spare time, I can tell you. One of my brothers went on to work at the Royal Mint in London.

My ancestors left money to buy bread for the poor and they also gave the ground and materials for the infants school to be built in Swan Lane, on condition that if ever it ceased to be a school the property should revert to the Druce family, but somehow we was done out of it. One of my grand-daughters wrote everywhere to try and get the property back. I think in the end the money from the sale of the old school went to the church authorities.

My gramp farmed Abbey Farm, one of the biggest in the village. And my dad told me that my aunt, Marion Druce, gave the communion rails for the church, brass they were, but in time they were taken down and wooden ones put in their place. And I had two maiden aunts who used to live in a nice house in Newland Street, called Blankstone, and they kept what they called 'the bag'. It contained day gowns, night gowns, back flannels, and napkins, in fact everything suitable for a newborn baby; there was also a half pound block of washing soap. You see, there were lots of people living here who were so poor that they couldn't afford to buy anything new for a baby. So my aunts had this idea, to keep 'the bag', and anyone in the village who had a baby could borrow it for two weeks. The soap was provided so that the mother could wash the clothes and send them back nice and clean.

I remember Harriet James telling me that a sure cure for rheumatism of the knees was to lay purple sprouting cabbage on them. Mind you, I've never tried it so I don't know whether it works or not.

Ah, this was a lovely friendly village years ago, now you hardly know your next-door neighbours.

41 The Square, Eynsham. Two of the Ovenall boys are included in the group.

❧ HILDA MAY COOLING ❧
née STEVENS *born* 1908

My parents first came to the village to live when I was about three years old. My father was a master baker and he had had his training at Abingdon.

When they took over the corn merchant's and bakehouse in Eynsham, the shop was only selling chicken and pig food, but gradually my mother, who ran the shop, started to sell groceries. Mind you, this upset the other shopkeepers in the village, I can tell you. The house was quite big, and many many years ago it had been the manor house.

My father and Foster Dore worked in the bakehouse, baking the bread, and sometimes my father made wedding cakes – they were his speciality, and he was classed as a master baker and confectioner. In the afternoons they would turn round and deliver bread in Eynsham, Cassington and Worton and Barnard Gate, while Hall's, one of the other bakers in the village, would deliver at Stanton Harcourt and Sutton. And, of course, my mother also sold bread in the shop.

At one time there were five bakers in the village, no wonder most of them had a sideline. Like a couple of other bakers, we sold coal. If a customer lived near then the coal would be delivered in a wheelbarrow, either by my father or Foster Dore. We also had a horse and cart for coal deliveries and another for bread.

When they took the bread down the Oxford road, they never paid to take the horse and cart through the toll gate. No, they used to tie the horse to the railings on the Eynsham side of the bridge. Then my father and Foster would load their wicker baskets up to the brim with loaves and carry them over to eight cottages, all with big families, that lay just over the Berkshire border. One day they had a very frisky young horse who was in the shafts for the first time. When they got back from delivering their bread to the cottages, the toll keeper, who stuttered, said to them 'I-I th-thought the bug-bugger wa-was go-going to-to ju-jump the blood-bloody ga-gate, he-he's bi-bin fra-francying a-about ev-ever sin-since y-you bi-bin go-gone.'

Every Sunday morning Mr Ashton, who was always called Per-Pan by the villagers, I don't know why, well he used to come and put a 'bottom' in the bakehouse oven. This was really to replace any bricks that might have got

42 One of the first bakers' vans to be owned by W. J. Stevens, master baker.

broken and crumbled away with the heat during the week.

My mother was very enterprising in her way. She used to make rice puddings in big round lard tins and sell the cold pudding for tuppence a lump. And bread puddings she made too, with the stale bread that was over in the bakehouse. This too she sold at tuppence a lump. And very often mothers would come in and buy both lumps of rice and bread pudding for their childrens' dinner.

When the First World War started Foster was called up, but then he got his discharge badge which he always wore in his lapel. So when my father was called up Foster did the baking: my mother would open the shop in the mornings, then turn round and help with delivering the bread in the afternoon. One day she was driving the pony and bread cart to Barnard Gate and suddenly the pony stopped dead and out went Mother straight on to the grass verge. She thought at the time that something must have shot over the road in front of the pony to make him suddenly stop like that.

At the end of the war my father came back and did the baking again. My mother concentrated on the shop, and I helped her out.

Between the wars we did very well, and in time the horses and carts were replaced by motor vehicles. We had a van, maroon it was, with W. J. Stevens boldly painted on the side. My father bought it from Phil Blake, and it had solid tyres and we were that proud of it, and of course we had a lorry to deliver the coal in as well.

We used to get a lot of 'sick and poor' tickets, value two shillings. The vicar

43 During the Second World War, Hilda Stevens and Baker Dore were responsible for running Stevens's bakery following her father's death. The bread was stacked in the back yard before being loaded into the van for delivery round Eynsham and Cassington.

44 Hilda Stevens and her mother dressed for their parts in a play entitled *Sherwood's Green*.

45 Eynsham Fair penny donkey ride. Hilda
Stevens's mother with a village youngster; the
donkey man looks on.

would issue these tickets to the very hard-up folk in the village. The money
really came from the charities fund, and the people who had them could only
spend them on food, though some would try and get a tupenny packet of
Woodbines out of Mother, but she would have no nonsense and they were
refused fags. A couple of times a year the vicar also used to give my father a
list, to deliver two hundredweight of coal: again these were to the very poor
people in the village, and again the bill was paid by the charities, St Thomas's
I believe it was called.

Of course over the years the price of coal and bread had risen out of all
proportion. In 1934 a ton of coal cost £1.18.0. but by 1935 it cost £2.3.4.,
and the same year ten loaves cost 3s. 1½d., that's threepence three farthings
each. And round about that time my father sold and delivered three loads of
manure for £1.10.0., I expect this was from our own horse.

During the Second World War my father died and we carried on for a
while. We managed with baker Dore and myself doing the baking and we
had a girl called Helen Clarke in the shop. She was a marvellous worker and
we shouldn't have been able to manage so long if it hadn't been for her. Then
she was about to leave and get married so mother and I decided to sell out.
I had already strained my heart lugging the dough about and Foster Dore
was getting old, so I suppose it was all for the best.

HAROLD A. QUAINTON

born 1908

My father was born at No. 80 Acre End Street, Eynsham, in 1882 and, according to him, when he left the Eynsham Board School, he became apprenticed to a Mr Davey, who had a business in a house in what is now Lord's Row. They worked for the farmers in the village and round about, collecting and delivering mended, and sometimes new, harness in a pony and cart.

In those days the harness maker was a very important member of the community, responsible for keeping the horses on the farms at work.

By now my father had married Miss Ellen Clark, a stonemason's daughter of Eynsham, and they set up home at No. 5 Crown Crescent, where I, their eldest son, was born in 1908. Round about this time Mr Davey died, and my father was persuaded to start his own business by the farmers, and by a Mr Thomas Hall, the local baker, coal merchant and grocer. Mr Hall helped my father to start up in the cottage in Crown Crescent. There was only a gentleman's agreement between them. Mr Hall paid my father's bills for leather, flock, buckles, and all other trade materials, and my father paid him back whenever he could do so. This arrangement lasted for many years, until Mr Hall died.

Around 1918–19 we were still living at No. 5 Crown Crescent. My mother now had six children – according to our family Bible she had three children in three years. I had been sent to live with my grandparents in 1910 and lived there until 1918, when my grandmother died and I came home. My mother's main concern always was to feed us, and I remember her getting meat bones and offal from Hedges' the butcher's shop – at the corner of Swan Lane – to boil up to make gravy. Any solid she used to make into brawn and these, with bread and potatoes and an occasional cake, seemed to sustain us. Mother did her cooking on a coal-fired stove. We only had candles for lighting at night. The toilet was a bucket type down the bottom of the garden, which a Mr Edwards used to empty.

At Christmas time our mother always managed to have a line strung across the room, usually with a few sugar fancies tied to it. Above all this hardship, neighbourly kindness from village people helped to sustain us. I remember two elderly neighbours, a Mrs Dickins and a Mrs Evans, very often gave us children a cake or a slice of bread and lard. Mr Hall was always in the background, along with Dr Cruikshank, Nurse Hathaway and the Revd William Nash Bricknell. In those days there was, of course, no state help, but people seemed to be always ready and willing to help each other.

By now a larger house was imperative and with help we moved into the large house in Mill Street (now Harriss's the butchers). For the first time we had a proper flush toilet, but no bathroom. Bathing still meant sitting in a zinc tray in front of the fire. My father's shop was in the large front room facing Mill Street. But above all we had more room: outside there were stables and a large loft where Mr Hall used to keep sacks of flour. All this happened around 1919. My brother William, mother's last child, was born there in 1921.

Father worked very hard in those days, with only a pushbike to get around on. Few farmers would deliver and fetch their repaired harness, and he had to cycle to them to fetch the harness, including collars and saddles. He had a way of loading his bike with two collars hanging each side from a carrier over the back wheel, and usually a saddle on top and smaller pieces of harness on the handlebars. Besides Eynsham a lot of his work came from the Stanton Harcourt, Standlake and Northmoor areas. Very occasionally, when harness work had built up at the farms, he would take his tools and work in the farm barns.

Father had large white leather hides hung up in his shop from which he made hedging cuffs, thongs for the farm carters' boots, and heavy stitching leather for horse collars and saddles etc. For stitching he used large curved needles with a steel palm tool which he pushed the needles in with. The tool was shaped into a tapered solid end about 2″ long and $\frac{3}{4}$″ in diameter; this had a hole in the end large enough to take his large curved needles, and he used it to pull the needle through. In harvest time, to make a change, father would sometimes help out a farmer friend with wheat loading and working with a steam-driven threshing box.

Besides harness-making, father had another skill – that of rope-making and tarpaulin sheet-making. He had been taught these in his early life by an old navy man named Jim Wall who used to live with my grandmother at 80 Acre End Street. In those days the rope walk was just above 80 Acre End Street, where I believe a Mr Ayres now lives. My father then set up his own rope walk at 80 Acre End Street. He fitted up a rope-making jack at the top of the garden (the jack is now in the County Museum, Woodstock) and, depending on the length of rope, the other end of the twine was attached to what father called a donkey, a heavy piece of timber about 6′ long, 9″ wide and 4″ thick, with two small iron wheels, about 6″ in diameter, fitted at the front. Above this was a stout upright wooden post, with an iron handle fitted at the top for turning a hook to which twine was attached. Sometimes the donkey was weighed down with a half cwt weight – I think this depended on the tightness of twist required. When the jack was turned the attached twines started to twist up, and this would pull the donkey gently along. There were normally three lines of twisted twine about $\frac{1}{4}'' \times \frac{3}{8}''$ thick, depending on the thickness of rope required: these were attached to the jack and made a cone shape at the hook on the donkey. My father then used a dolly – a piece of hardwood about 6″ long and 4″ in diameter, slightly tapered at one end, with rounded grooves cut into it to take the twisted twine. Father would position the dolly near the hook on the donkey with the three twisted twines in the dolly grooves. Now the moment had arrived for the finished rope to leave the dolly, with the donkey gently moving along behind. A lot of the rope father made was used for plough lines.

About 1922–3, Mr Roland Harris, the village blacksmith, bought the Mill Street property for his son to live in, and of course that meant another move for us. Father managed to rent a cottage two doors down from Mr Tichell's shop, and practically opposite over the road he rented for his workshop a small room facing the road, from Mr Butler, the landlord of The Jolly Sportsman. These were certainly not ideal conditions, but we soon adapted.

By 1922 our family of seven were growing up. School meant first going to the Infant School in Swan Street, and then on to the Board School in Witney Road. The headmaster was a Cornishman, Mr J. T. Trethewy – a good headmaster and a disciplinarian. His wife was headmistress for the girls. Looking back, I have a lot to thank the headmaster for. He gave me a good start in life. In those days the Revd Nash Bricknell used to visit the school every Friday to pay him his salary.

In Christmas 1922 I left school at fourteen years of age, and of course a job of work was essential to help with the family budget. My first job, lasting about six weeks, was to help our milkman, Mr Jesse Treadwell; he lived in Mill Street, and worked at Franklin's farm, the Oxford side of the tollgate. My job was to help him push the milk cart from the farm to Eynsham. The milk cart was made of wood: it had two large wheels at the side, and one small wheel in the front, and a large milk churn was suspended in the middle. It was an awful struggle to get up the railway bridge and the incline and into Eynsham. I often wonder how Jesse used to manage on his own.

By now father had arranged for me to be apprenticed as a plumber with the Oxford firm of T. H. Kingerlee & Sons, where my grandfather had worked as a carpenter and wheelwright. I was apprenticed through the Eynsham Bartholomew Charity. For the next twenty years I cycled to Oxford and back to get to work: I had a permanent job with a good employer for the next fifty years.

Father stayed in The Jolly Sportsman workshop until around 1930, always busy with the harness repairs – and with a new job of making and repairing binder canvasses. These were used on the harvesting machines when the wheat, oats, barley etc. were cut. The binder canvas was about 6' wide and fitted with ash lathe which were tacked and rivetted to the canvas about every 9". It revolved around rollers, carrying the corn into the machine where it was bound into sheafs with binder twine and then thrown out for stooking up into pyramid-shaped stacks. I remember the dreadful unemployment at this time. Father usually had local men sitting in his workshop watching him work: it was company for him, and there were not a lot of facilities for the unemployed in those days.

In the early 1930s father had a lucky break in so far as he was able to rent No. 1 Crown Crescent. This was wonderful, since he was able to use the front room for his workshop again, while mother had plenty of room at the back, although the W.C. was at the top of the garden and the sink in the outside washhouse. By now the family was growing up. Three of my sisters were in domestic service and away from home, and the rest of us, except my young brother William, were at work. By the mid 1930s the farm tractor was gradually beginning to affect my father's harness work, but such is life that when one door closes, another opens. He already had a lot of experience with rope making and canvas work, and as the local canvas- and tarpaulin-maker, Mr Fred Ford of Corn Street, Witney, had passed away, my father was constantly being asked by the local farmers for canvas tarpaulins, especially during the harvest and haymaking seasons. Father was able to rent the loft at The Jolly Sportsman. He had large bench-top tables and trestles made and generally adapted the large loft for a very busy part of his job – so much so that he was able to employ a Mr Billie Betterton of Eynsham, an experienced man who had previously worked for Mr Ford of Witney. All the canvas stitching was done by hand, and the holding down ropes father made himself, splicing the ends of them after passing them through the brass eyelets. He cut his own stencils, sometimes from newspaper, for putting the customers' names on the tarpaulins, and of course he always printed his own name on them.

The tarpaulin side of his job gradually became the major part of his work as the horses disappeared from the farms and the tractors took over. Besides the farmers' requirements he made tarpaulins for industrial firms like Smith's of Witney and Pressed Steel, Cowley, for use on their transport vehicles. These were certainly better times for my mother and father, and they seemed to get their enjoyment from this work. I don't ever remember them going to a cinema or a theatre: a big event was an occasional Sunday excursion from Eynsham railway station to Southsea. Sometimes they used to put their best clothes on – father with his bowler hat – and walk to The Star public house, Witney Road, and have a drink with my wife and me and my other brothers and sisters that could make it. Life for them was very much the same until December 1954, when my father had to go to the Radcliffe Infirmary for what is now a simple operation. This was the first time mother and father had been parted all through their married life. He recovered from the operation, but passed away when he was seventy-two years old. He went on working right up to the time of his admission to hospital.

This was a terrible shock to my mother, but as the months passed she gradually adapted herself with the love and help of her six remaining children. My brother Reginald sadly lost his life in Holland fighting for his country in 1942.

From December 1954 until December 1973 mother kept her home going, and was very determined to live on her own. She managed quite well for around fifteen years with help from my sisters Rita and Joan, who live in the village, and her doctor and friend Dr Bolsover. From then onwards her legs gave her a lot of trouble, partly immobilizing her and causing quite a lot of pain, but she never complained. One of the joys of mother keeping her home going was that it became a meeting place for her children and kept the family together. She loved to see us all, and always made us welcome, usually with a cup of tea and a mince pie, whatever the time of year.

Sadly in December 1973 mother passed away, aged ninety-one years, loved and missed very much by her children. Her wish was to be laid to rest with my father in Eynsham churchyard.

❧ JIM EVANS ❧
born 1897

I was born a twin. My twin sister died at birth and I was dying too, so my mother told me. So they sent for the vicar, as my mother wanted me christened before I died. Well, he come into the kitchen, took one look at me and said, 'I shall want a drop of water.' So my eldest sister was sent out to the old well in the garden to draw some up. She brought some in in a basin and the vicar did his stuff, you know, marked me forehead with a cross and from then on I thrived and I reckon I've had a charmed life, and all through being christened with a drop of well water.

Ten of us there was in family and we was as poor as church mice. Other people used to give us their old clothes, we never knowed what it was to have new ones. My mother used to go out and do half a day's washing for sixpence and a small basin of dripping. All the washing was done by hand, rubbing and scrubbing to get the clothes clean, and boiling it up in the old fire copper afterwards.

Sometimes we would come home from school at dinner times and there would be nothing for us to eat. All our young lives we reckoned that we had more dinner times than dinners. If the red cloth was on the table we knowed there was nothing to eat. Then our mother would go out to the garden and pick a few greens or brussel sprouts and we would be sent down with the cabbage to Mrs Wall. And in exchange she would give us a cup of 'frying pan dripping'. All colours that dripping was where she had used it for cooking different things. Then we would go over to Biggers's the baker and ask for a 2½*d.* loaf. It would be booked down of course, and if she had any money our mother would pay for it, and the rest of the bread we'd had that week, on Saturday. Well that would be our dinner, bread and dripping – ah, many a time we've had that. And sometimes we would have just bread with a sprinkling of sugar on for our dinner. And often we had tea with neither milk nor sugar in. You see my father was a hay tyer, casually employed, so when it rained, it was a case of 'no work, no pay'.

Course living conditions in our cottage was pretty grim. Cold stone floors and broken bedroom floors. You could see down into the kitchen through the floor boards. The old lavatory was right down the bottom of the garden, and if you wanted to go in the night, that was it, you had to put your trousers on and go out in the cold, there was nothing else for it. There was no proper pavements or anything like that in the village, muddy roads and muck everywhere. Just inside the door of our cottage was a sack-bag folded in two, that was to wipe your dirty boots on. Mind you in fine weather the sack-bag was always put outside on the doorstep. Most people had a sack-bag to wipe their boots on, only the better off had scrapers outside their houses.

When we was kids we got up to all sorts of capers. Once me and two of my brothers, our Jack and our Bert, called at a Mrs Dingle's house. She felt sorry for us as a family and nearly always gave us a slice of bread and dripping or a bit of stale cake. Anyhow she give us a parcel, wrapped in newspaper it was. When we got up the lane we opened it and inside was a raw bullock's heart. Well we gnawed a few bites each off it and then decided to hide it until the next day when we could finish it off. So we hid it in the stinging nettles. Quite early next day we goes shooting off down the Station Road to claim our bullock's heart. But overnight the slugs had got at it, it was covered in 'um so we couldn't eat it.

During the early part of the war there were troops stationed nearby at Swinford, the Lancers I think they were. Well, one day we lads finds some tins of bully beef hid, we reckoned that they had been put there for somebody to pick up. Do you know we tried all manners of ways to open one of them tins, we bashed it against the toll bridge wall without any success. You see we was afraid to take 'um home in case we met the copper, 'cos he would chase you for nothing.

One day we boys was sitting in a manger at Cockerell's Farm, just chatting and doing no harm. In come the policeman, he gets out his truncheon and comes for us. We ducked and leapt over the double doors, down over the railway line, with him running after us. We went to the 'paddles' or the weir, which is on the old canal. We stopped down there till it was dark, laying in the long grass. We was frightened to go home till it was pitch dark in case he was waiting for us.

When I was about ten years old I used to help deliver the bread for one of the bakers on Saturdays. We would go off with the pony and cart all round the surrounding villages, getting back about half past nine. For this the baker would give me 3d. I'd go into Pimm's, the nearest shop, and buy a candle, a bundle of kindling wood and a box of matches for a ha'penny each. These was to take home for my mother. That left me three ha'pence for meself. Straight to Polly Walls I'd go and buy a pen'orth of cold rice pudding, and then a ha'pence-worth of scrumps from a man who used to come on Saturday nights and sell fish and chips. The fish was tuppence and a portion of chips a penny. But these scrumps was the little bits of crisp batter that fell off the fish as it was being cooked. He served the scrumps in a little white pointed bag. I used to sprinkle plenty of vinegar on and when I'd finished I used to tip that three-cornered bag up and drink the vinegar. Oh, that was lovely!

There were lots of small shops and tradespeople in our village when I was young, where you could buy all manner of things. Of course the shops catered for everybody's needs and at least two of them sold everything from a bike to a box of matches. Not many folk bothered to go into Oxford. You could go on the carrier's cart for fourpence, or he would bring back shopping from Oxford, charging tuppence for carriage. He'd bring you anything, elastic, ladies' bloomers, combs and things, he didn't mind. On appro. he would bring, say, three pairs of boots from Freeman, Hardy & Willis, taking back the ones you didn't want next time he went to Oxford. Then there was the train – you could go to Oxford and back for ninepence, but not many could afford that.

There was even a bike shop here, you could hire a bike for sixpence an hour so as you could learn to ride,* and Tricky Wilkins would let you hire one a week for half a crown, so that you could ride to work. This was marvellous really, because it took such a long time to save for even a second-hand bike. In the newspapers at that time I remember seeing that Gamages of London were advertising new bikes for £2.10.0., but who in the world had got that much?

Once me and one of my brothers was on our allotment, clearing up and burning the rubbish. Well, the man on the next allotment didn't like it and he started shouting at us. Course we cheeked him and he started to chase us shouting, 'You cheeky young varmints, I'll cut yer bloody heads awf if I catches you.' So we ran like billyho and was nearly home, I was in front and my brother trailing a bit behind, when this man fired a shot gun at my brother and hit him in the thigh. I went rushing back and the blood was oozing out, so I runs indoors and eldest sister said she'd come. She picked my brother up in her arms and run down to the doctor's with him. The doctor said he ought to go to hospital Of course, there was no hospital transport in them days, so we goes into Biggers's the bakers and asks if we can borrow their pony and cart. But we had to go down to the field and catch the pony first. Anyway we got no money to take him the quickest way round through the toll-gate – the A.40 wasn't built till 1934 – so we had to go the long way

* Other reports say 3d. an hour.

46 Jim Evans's father-in-law cutting grass with a cutting machine: the toll bridge and the River Thames are in the background.

47 Cutting and baling the hay. The group consists of Percy Harper, Jim Ayres, Bunny Ayres and Harry Higgs. All of them worked for H. O. King – as did Jim Evans and his father.

round through Cassington and Yarnton. Anyway Harry soon got better; its the breeding you see, we Evans's are tough.

Another old fellow who had an allotment near ours was having trouble with hares getting on his land and eating his greenstuff. So he sets a trap to try and catch 'um. When he arrived one evening he could hear a hare squealing, it had just been caught in the trap and was trying to get out. Now when a hare squeals it sounds just like a human being crying over and over again, 'I ain't, I ain't.' 'Oh yes you have, you old bugger,' the man said, ' 'Cos I've caught you at it, and you ain't going to get out of this trap alive.'

During the wintertimes we used to go off bird catching with birds nets or clap nets as some folks call 'um. Blackies and thrushes and sometimes a pheasant if we was lucky. When we did get a pheasant we would take it to old Bob Buck who kept one of the pubs in the village and sell it to him. Course we never really had the proper price for 'um. The cunning old devil would hold the bird up by the legs and say 'Ah, 'es a waster, I'll give 'ee two shillings for him.' But the thrushes and blackbirds we would take home and our mother would soon have the feathers off and we would have a nice pie with them.

We played all sorts of games, in the street of course as there was little or no traffic. 'Whips and tops', 'marbles', 'sheep sheep come home', 'please I've come to learn the trade', and 'playing plancher'. That was a sort of hunt the thimble, only it was played with a piece of crock – a broken bit of a cup. The one that was 'it' hid this piece of crock in the crevices of a stone wall, and the others had to try and find it, with the one that was 'it' telling them if they were hot or cold when they got near. The one that found it then became 'it'. Ah, we would play that game for hours.

When I was thirteen I got a job on a farm, in wintertime it was, and I had to be there at six o'clock in the morning 'hiking' up the cows, that's calling them in from the fields. There was just one hurricane lamp in the cowshed, that was the only light to do the milking by – all hand-milking of course.

Old Jessie, the fellow that I worked with, would say, 'You have that 'un, course you'll have to tie his legs or he'll kick the hell out of you.' Other jobs I had was grinding up the swedes and mangolds for the cattle. You put the stuff in the swede grinder, which was something like a very big mincer and turned the handle for it to work. Quite a lot of farm workers lost part of a finger that way, you know, they would put their hand in to stuff the swedes down turning the handle at the same time and, bingo, the top of their finger was off.

And once I had a job helping Ben Ayres and Joe Pratley. They were cutting the rushes in the river Windrush, from Witney to Standlake, to clear the river you see. First of all scythe blades were bolted together and a rope fixed on each side. With Ben Ayres on one side of the river and Joe Pratley on the other they would walk along, pulling the scythe to and fro, cutting the rushes as they went. Beforehand they would have fixed willow poles across the river at different points, to sort of dam the rushes and stop them floating off too far. My job was to heave the rushes out of the river. For this I used a tool which was called a 'dung drag'. I had to make ricks on the river bank of the cut rushes, and I think it was the hardest job that I ever had. I got two pounds a week for this, only the last week we was unlucky, none of us had any wages at all, because the man in charge had gone off with it.

Oh, I've had all sorts of jobs in my time. For a little while I worked in Oxford at a tobacconist's for six shillings a week. Then my father got me a job with him hay-tying. We worked for a man called H. O. King whose slogan to his workmen was

> If not pressed and tied with string,
> You'll do no more for H. O. King.

The tools that were needed for this job were a hay knife, a hay rake, a hay fork or pitchfork, a hay pin, to hold the hay together, a paring knife to trim up the trusses, a talacre – which was a blue stone to sharpen the knives with – and a grindstone, or grinstun', as my father called it. This was a round sharpening stone fixed on a piece of iron with a handle on, and it was my job to turn the handle round and round to sharpen the big hay knife.

We had to walk miles often to the field where the hay ricks were. But first we had to borrow a horse to take the hay press, which belonged to Mr King, to where we were to work, and borrow a ladder too. When the ladder was set up against the rick, I had to shin up it and remove all the thatch from the rick before we could make a start. Then my father would go to the top of the rick and start cutting the hay with a very big hay knife, three foot six inches long they were. The hay was cut from the rick in huge trusses, about 56 lb each. Then my father had to carry these, on his head, from the top of the rick to the ground, so that his mates could start to press and tie it. It was very hard work, pressing the great lever down to get the bale good and firm. One rick might contain forty tons of hay, and we had to cut and press and tie it and stack it four bales wide and five high for four shillings a ton. Two tons a day one man and one boy could do. Then we had to load it up when the horses and carts came to take it away. And sometimes we had to put loads on rail – 108 haybales we used to stack in one railway truck.

Mind you the work wasn't all local, and I remember I had to stay in lodgings when we worked at Wheatley, twelve miles away. Another time we lodged at Alvescote, a matter of ten miles away, walking back home at the weekend across the fields pinching swedes and turnips from the farmers' fields, gnawing the skin off and then eating them we was that hungry. We used to carry our bit of grub in a 'flagging' basket. This was a basket made from rushes, cut from the river locally and made by Tom Skinner. A bit of bread and cheese or fat bacon and a bottle of cold tea, that's all you had to last you all day long.

We used to go straw tying as well, but it was quite different to hay tying. Here you raked or 'hatched' the straw into a heap and made your bale like that, but you didn't press it as tight as you did hay, and the straw was often tied with 'bonded straw', which we made ourselves by twisting the straw, then the ties were tightened up with a pair of twisters.

Then Vincent Ayres got me a job on the farm, to better meself. This was at Woolstan near Coventry. I went off by train, the only luggage I'd got was a cardboard box which held me Sunday boots. My working ones that had cost 4s. 6d. was as hard as china, especially after you had walked through the wet grass in 'um and tried to dry 'um. Anyhow 'twas a terrible job, I hated it. Hoeing peas in the boiling sun all day and the ground was as hard as concrete. Well, I stuck it a week, got me pay and decided to go home. I waited till dark then leapt over the wall, and I picked up a handful of stones to throw at anybody who might come after me. I walked twelves miles to Leamington Station, after sleeping all night in somebody's coalhouse.

I got on the train for Oxford and when I reached there I'd just got my fare to Eynsham and one penny over so I had a bar of Swiss milk chocolate out of one of those machines on the platform and caught the half-past-sevener home.*

During the early part of the First World War I got a job in Birmingham at the Fort Dunlop factory helping to make solid bike and motor bike tyres, then in 1917 I volunteered for the army and was in the Field Artillery for a couple of years. I had tried to join earlier but had been turned down as unfit, but by 1917 they'd lost that many men, they was glad of anybody. I was demobbed in 1919, so it was back to the old village again.

Well, I had the chance to buy a big bass drum from John Picket, he used to beat it for the Salvation Army. I'd already got a little side drum. My brother William, always known as 'sniper' because that's what he had been when he served with the Oxon & Bucks, well he had got a gramophone and

* The 'half-past-sevener' was the local name for the evening train.

[117]

48 Jim Evans's father-in-law using one of the first reaping (binding) machines in the area.

49 Jim Evans (standing on the far right) in the Field Artillery.

we'd got a few records between us, so along with our brother Jack we sets up as a dance band, 'Sergeant Evans's Jazz Band'. And we was ever so popular for dances and social functions, in the village and the surrounding ones. We even helped to start Eynsham carnival and paraded round the streets with the gramophone on a hand cart.

After a while I got a super job as chauffeur driving a Rolls Royce car. The car had been specially made for this Indian prince and princess and I had to drive them all over the place in it. Mostly they stopped at the Grand Hotel at Brighton, and if the fancy took them they would get me to drive them up to London, just to go to the pictures or theatre. One day, I was going off to pick them up and I was in a bit of a hurry when suddenly a young lad came out of a turning on a bike, I cut both boy and bike flying. Fortunately the boy wasn't hurt but the bike was damaged. Quick as a flash I said to the lad 'Take the number, I got royalty aboard', got back in the car and drove off at speed. Anyway I never heard no more about it. After that I had several different jobs, road-making and lorry-driving. You see by then I was married with a daughter, so I got to work nearer home. My wife was a wonderful person, country born and bred, she could make a meal out of almost nothing.

My wife used to tell me about her first job of work after leaving school at thirteen. She was sent out to service on a farm at Southleigh and, although it was only about four miles from her home she had to 'sleep out' at the place where she was employed. Of course the wages were terrible, two shillings a week and her board. As she did not own any house shoes or slippers, her employers bought her some, but she had no wages for two weeks, they took that to pay for the shoes. Another thing, they always expected her to go to church every Sunday. In time she got a bit fed up with this and happened to mention the fact to the cowman's wife. 'Ah, you come along yer and set with I, they won't know no difference,' she said. So come Sunday she went straight to the cowman's cottage and sat with his wife until it was time for the folk to come out of church. Then she began to panic – 'What if they asks me what the text was, what be I going to say?' The cowman's wife was evidently 'a bit fly', as we calls folks that are on the bright side: 'You tell 'um it was, "behold I went not" – that way you won't be telling a lie, will you?'

Do you know, I never earned more than £14 a week in my life, and that was since the Second World War – before then I worked for two and three pounds a week. But I did manage to buy the cottage we lived in down by the toll-bridge at Swinford and two more besides a bit later on. I've been retired now since 1966. But I'm still a river bailiff for the Oxford Angling Club, have been for over thirty years, and I'm very interested in local history and often

50 Jim Evans in chauffeur's uniform when he was driving a Rolls Royce for an Indian prince and his wife. The photograph was taken at Brighton.

give a talk to groups in the village about how we managed when we were young. I lost my wife in 1979, but I remarried in 1981. I've got lots of friends in the village too and we spend a lot of time talking about the 'good old days'. Hard up but happy days, and if I had the chance, I wouldn't have had it any different.

⊸ EMILY BOLTON ⊱
née PIMM *born* 1891

My grandfather, on my mother's side, was Henry Mathews, the Baptist minister here for several years. One of my forbears was standard-bearer to King Edward I, and my great-grandfather was the last Earl of Llandaff.

My mother used to tell us of the healing properties that her father Henry Mathews had. One woman who lived down Queen Street went to him in great pain. He fetched out his pure silk handkerchief, laid it where the pain was, and prayed; then he removed the scarf, and the pain was gone. He often did things like that. My mother used to say that it was a mixture of faith and prayer that did it. Years before coming to our village he had lived as a teacher in America. While there he was asked to engrave an American dollar bill. Another of his accomplishments was to paint a book of butterflies; his book is now in the British Museum, and on the back inside page is a copy of the dollar bill he was asked to engrave.

When he came to Eynsham he started a school in the Bartholomew School Room in the Square, charging tuppence a week for each pupil. This was of course before either the National or the Infants' School were built.

I am the fourth of a family of twelve – there are only eight of us left now. My mother was ninety-five when she died. She and father brought us all up, as well as running the village store all her life. The shop was right in the centre of the village facing the church, and sold almost everything. Every item of grocery imaginable: hardware, ironmongery, meat, milk, oil, drapery – you name it, we sold it. We even kept cows as well. Jack Pickett used to look after them; they were kept in a field down Station Road. He used to milk them and bring the milk up to the shop in a big steel can.

One thing that my mother always sold in the shop was home-made rice pudding. It was made in great big oblong meat tins, using some of the milk from our cows, and then cooked in our big black range in the kitchen. This pudding, solid when it was done, was sold for a penny a lump. So solid was it that we just cut out squares and wrapped it in a bit of paper. I reckon many a child in the village owed their very existence to my mother's rice pudding.

Pigs too we kept, and again Jack Pickett looked after them. He worked for

51 Pimm's shop in the Square. This picture was taken before an extra shop had been built into the buildings on the far left.

52 A much later photograph of Pimm's shop, with Mrs Pimm – Emily Bolton's mother – standing outside. The extra shop can be seen on the left.

us all his life, from the time he left school till he died, and he could turn his hand to anything. When he killed a pig we used to plague him for the bladder so we could play football with it. We used to sell the fresh pigmeat in the shop – old Jack would mince up the pigs' lights and things and make beautiful faggots, then turn round and sell them round the villages at a penny a piece. And the lovely lard he used to make in a room above the shop that we always called 'the lard room'.

I can see him now mincing up the pigs' flear ready to make it, tipping the flear into a big black saucepan, over a coal fire. As soon as the fat started to run he would pour it off – the times he did this, setting the saucepan back over the flames, taking it off again as soon as he thought there was some melted in it, pouring it off into big steel pans. You had to do that when you made lard, otherwise the lard wouldn't keep white, but burn and go a fawny colour. Then he would put the pans of lard on one side to set. Funny – it was never quite smooth on the top, but slightly wavy, like a miniature white sea it looked. But the flavour of pure pigs' lard was magical. As well as selling it in the shop we used to eat it too. Spread thick on new bread, dusted either with salt or sugar according to one's taste. Ah lovely it was. And the little bits of cooked fat left over from the lard making were another treat, specially if we had the chance to eat them hot. Scratchings we called them, but some people called them crutlins or cruttons.

Do you know, my mother and a Mrs Gibbard were the first young women in the village to own a bicycle apiece. Years later we children had a man's bike, with a fixed wheel, that was shared between us, and five of us used to get on it at once and we would often ride in to Oxford on it – one sitting on the handlebars, one on the crossbar, one on the saddle, pedalling, and two on the fixed carrier on the back. We called the bike 'the Roman charger' and spent many happy hours playing on it.

Proper tomboys we girls were too. We wore long black stockings and button-up boots. When the stockings got holes in them, I never bothered to mend them, no, I used to black my skin where my white legs showed through with boot blacking and got away without mending them. We were such a big family and we children were known as the 'terrible Pimms' because we were always getting up to mischief. I remember one time when we got caught pinching Victoria plums up Abbey Street, where our father had his building and carpentry business. He was the only man in the village at that time who made coffins. Up there was a big sawpit where the men used to saw up great trees and wood of all sorts. It was a deep pit and one man had to work down there – one worked above ground and one below, one on each end of this great long saw. It was a nasty pit full of frogs and toads. Just next to this pit was a building with a sort of wooden window opening out to a garden (not ours), and if we pushed this window thing open there against it was this beautiful plum tree. We children made all sorts of excuses to go up to the pit when we knew the plums were ripe, so that we could open the window, push our small hands through and grab some plums. But one day the owner was sat in his garden waiting for us and grabbed one of my brother's hands and wouldn't let go till we promised never to do it again.

But it wasn't all playing. During the school holidays and weekends I often went to nearby Stanton Harcourt and Sutton, at nine years old mind you, to get and deliver orders. Jack Pickett would come with me just to drive and hold the pony and trap while I went into the cottages for orders. I could drive the pony and cart, but the pony we had at that time we called 'the eagle mare' and it was a bit frisky and would never stand quiet, so it needed somebody to be with it all the time. We also had a bigger 'buggy', as we called it. In fact it was a lovely horse-drawn covered cart with shelves all built in it on which we stacked all sorts of groceries and things. I suppose it really was a travelling shop, and it gave the housewives in the hamlets and villages a chance to *see* what they could buy. Bread and all we took round, this we fetched from Cox's bakehouse down Queen Street.

I was ten years old before I went to the National School. You see, all we Pimms went to a private school run by the Misses Pierce, two maiden ladies they were. The school was in a house in the High Street, next to the doctor's. One day the doctor said to our mother, 'I can't understand why you pay for all your children to go there, they would learn just as much if not more by going to the National School.' So that was it, we all left the Misses Pierce's and went to the National School – well the younger ones went to the Infants' School down Swan Lane, which was built on the site of an old cockfighting pit.

The headmistress at the Infants' at that time was a Mrs Buckingham, but the village children always called her 'Duke' Buckingham because she thought she was posh.

I remember the first time we ran outside our shop to watch a car go by. Solid tyres it had on, and you could hear it coming miles away, clouds of dust it kicked up too, but it was so exciting to watch this smelly monster, the first of many to come and to pass along in front of the shop.

When I was fourteen I became a pupil teacher. I taught for two years under Mrs Trethewy, who was headmistress at the big school (the National), but I got no pay for this. At that time it was considered a part of your training

53 Children at the Infants' School in 1912. Mrs Bolton – then Emily Pimm – taught there, and is second from the left at the back of the picture.

to become a teacher. Then I studied through Clough's correspondence college and passed, that was in 1910. I also went to night school at the Oxford Technical College to study Art. I was offered a scholarship there, but I couldn't take it because I hadn't got any money. So I went to the Infants' in Swan Lane to teach there. My wages were two and a half guineas a month. After a while I went up to the National School to teach there – my wages were £40 a year. I taught girls standard two and three, and it was very hard work.

I married my first husband at the outbreak of war. He came home on leave a couple of times and then was killed in 1916 in the trenches, and I was left with a daughter to bring up. Still, I went on with my teaching, and after the war I had the chance to go to America on a teaching scheme.

I did think that I might settle there. But when I came home and renewed a friendship with a young man who lived in the village, Charles Bolton, that was it. I decided to stay, and we got married. In the early days of our marriage I bought myself a motorbike – I was the first woman in the village to have one, a Mackenzie it was. There was no kick-start on it – you had to

[125]

54 Teachers at the Infants' School, 1912. Standing at the back, left to right, are Dorothy Buckingham and her mother, Mrs 'Duke' Buckingham, the headmistress. Seated are May Goodwin, Emily Pimm and Daisy Mantelo.

55 On the left is Mrs 'Duke' Buckingham; on the right is Mrs Hedges, wife of the local butcher.

run and push it to start and then fling your leg over the saddle. But the fashion at the time was for long, narrow skirts which made the action impossible, so I went into Oxford and got myself a pair of trousers made, and the locals thought I was terrible to wear such things. After a while I replaced the motor bike with a car; again I was the first woman in the village to own a car and be granted a licence to drive one. An Austin Seven it was – 'lost in Devon' we called them. Lovely little car it was too.

When we started to grow up my mother, sisters and I all wore dresses with stiffeners sewn into the neck to keep them stiff, and we wore long skirts which we picked up at one side as we walked along – to show an ankle and sometimes a bit of leg. But my husband didn't like me doing that. 'I don't mind seeing your legs,' he said, 'But I don't want anybody else to see them.'

Then a revelation in dress fashion came along – Peter Pan collars. Gone were the stiff, high, tight ones. Now necklines were lower, with nice round, soft, white collars which we tacked on to our dark dresses. Some of the collars were made of silk or linen or lace, and many girls crocheted their own. The first time my father saw me in one of these he was horrified. 'You looks all scrawky necked,' he said, having probably never seen my neck before. We made most of our own clothes using dozens of hooks and eyes to fasten the back of the tight-fitting dresses. Then press-fasteners came along, and that was a much nicer way of fastening up our clothes.

Although my grandfather had been the Baptist minister, in time we all went to the Apostolic Church in the village. We were always given to understand that a man called Irving started this sort of religion in this country. So we Pimms were always called 'Irvingites' by the locals. And at six o'clock on a Monday morning there was always a special service there. This was to start you off fresh for the working week. Well, one morning my brother George and I went to this service. Now if we went straight back home after the service we were expected to get the breakfast for all the family, so George and I decided that we would go for a cycle ride. Up the Witney Road we went.

Now there was a man in the village called Joe Ryan – poor man, not quite as he should have been. He always used to walk about the village with his hands behind his back talking to himself, and the children used to tease him and make him worse. Well, he got that bad that he was taken away to what was called the 'lunatic asylum' – there was nowhere else for anybody in that condition to go in those days. But on this Monday morning George and I both saw him just as he always was, walking along with his hands behind his back mumbling to himself, up the Witney Road just by Cox's barn it was. Well, when we got back we told mother that we had seen old Joe. 'You couldn't have,' she said, 'you know they took him away to the asylum weeks ago.' Later that day the local minister called at the shop and told my mother that old Joe had died – apparently at the very moment that we had seen him up by Cox's barn.

Of course the Apostolic Church is not used very much these days. My brother Bevan, who is a deacon there, takes a service now and then, and it is only members of the Pimm family who still attend.

Well, I've taught in many schools in the county, and when I was at Cogges school I developed several new teaching methods which were later taken up by the county. I was still a relief teacher when I was well in my seventies and people often come up to me and thank me for teaching them.

All through my life I have taken an interest in the village, belonging to a number of things including the Women's Institute, and for a while I was the W.I. President in Eynsham. And when I was over eighty I was still performing in the W.I. drama group. Our shop closed around 1972–3 and that part of the village has gone for ever. Some of the building is used as a self-service grocery mini-market, while another part is used as a launderette, and the end red-brick building, which my parents had built specially for drapery, is used as a china and stationer's shop and is still run by my brother Bevan and his family, so at least the name of Pimm is still there. Three of my brothers took up the building trade, and although my brother George is still alive, Pimm's the builders' firm is now run by his sons. There have been Pimms in the village for 600 years and I hope that there will be for the next 600 years.

❧ WILLIAM THOMAS GRANT ❧
born 1899

We lived at 4 Elm Cottages and our dad worked for Green's the builders. He was a bricklayer and never earned no more than thirty shillings a week, if that. There was seven of us in family, four girls and we three boys, and we was hard up, we sin more dry bread than anything else I can tell you. Mind you we did have a bit of something on our bread when it run to it.

Bread and lard ('starve guts' was the local name for it), ah we loved bread and lard, especially when you was allowed to sprinkle a bit of sugar on it, though some folks like it with salt sprinkled on. And when our mother could afford the sugar she would make jam – you know, blackberry, crab and apple, and when there was a glut of plums she'd make them into jam too. Pozzy, that was our name for jam always. And although cheese was cheap we never had a lot of that, our dad did of course and his favourite slang word for cheese was 'bung 'ole', though to tell you the truth it always had the opposite effect on me.

Mrs Buckingham and Mary Goodwin was the teachers at the Infants' School down Swan Lane. It didn't matter about being a scholar, at seven years old you was sent up to the big school. Mr Trethewy was a good teacher, well he was headmaster. And if you done anything wrong in the lower classes they told Mr Trethewy and he'd come down and give you four stripes with his cane. It was no good you saying as you would tell your parents, he'd take no notice of that. I left school at twelve, in them days them let you go.

No, we never had much grub as kids nor no clothes neither, only other folks' left-offs.

One day the vicar said to our mam, 'You bring young Bill along to church next Sunday' – course 'twas only a catch to get me to join the choir. Once you had joined you had to go to church every Sunday morning and night and choir practice every Thursday, and we boys had a clout round the earhole if we didn't go.

One Christmas we choir boys set off on our annual carol singing lark. We was allowed, as members of the choir, to go and sing carols at all the big houses and farms at Christmastime – it was a lovely clear moonlight night too. Off we goes right up to Farmer Dean's at Twelve Acres, we sung three carols there, and then cut across to Barnard Gate right up the drive to Eynsham Hall park to Squire Mason's. Well, before we gets to Mason's we comes to a big tall hedge and one of the older boys says 'What about a fag then?' Lord only knows where they got 'um from. So we all lights up, and then we starts puffing and coughing like a lot of old men. Suddenly a voice says 'All right, stay where you are, I've caught you red-handed.' Damn me if it wasn't the local copper, name of Jones. Strikes me hed bin a-following us all the way and we didn't know it. Then he said 'What made you think that nobody would know as you was smoking, I see this big black cloud a-rising up over this yer hedge and I thought that's them young varmints from the church choir, and I was right wasn't I?'

And do you know we all had to go to Witney before the court and we was summonsed five shillings each, so bang went our carol singing money. I was only twelve at the time – smoking under age, they said.

We never had proper bikes of our own, but if we could get a few bits and pieces that other folk had throwed away we'd make ourselves up a bit of a bike, mind you, there'd be no mudguards or fancy things like that on 'um. They was only old crocks really.

At that time thur was a man in the village called Leo Browne, he used to do bikes up and sell 'um. He was quite good to we boys and he'd give us odd bits as was no good to him and we would use 'um on our old bikes. He knew damned well as we should never be able to afford to buy anything off him. And I remember he had a big painted sign nailed up on the wall of his cottage, down the Oxford Road he lived, and this is what was written on there –

STOP!

Here lives the man who'd ne'er refuse
To mend all kinds of inner tubes
All kinds of cycles he'll repair
And only charge you what is fair
He'll mend a puncture in your tyre
Or let you out a bike on hire
The lot is good and the work is just
The profits are small, so cannot trust.

There was a rumour going round that the police had got their eye on him because they suspected that he was mixed up with some pushbikes that had been stolen, and then he had done 'um up so as nobody should recognize 'um and then sold 'um. Our Mam said to us 'Don't you take nothing else off that

Mr Browne, it might have been pinched, and they'd have you up the top of Witney [police court] afore you could say Jack Robinson.' But soon after these rumours had been flying round, Mr Browne left the village.

Then seventeen or eighteen years after, we villagers had the shock of our lives. Apparently this same Leo Browne and his accomplice, a Mr William Kennedy, was stopped by a policeman because he suspected them of being in possession of a stolen Morris Cowley car. This was on the road between Romford and Ongar. Well, one of the men shot and injured the policeman, then before they drove off one of them shot him in the eyes, you see folk at that time believed that the reflection of a murderer could be seen in a dead man's eyes, that's why they shot his eyes out, which of course killed him.

I tell 'ee the village was all agog when they read about it in the papers and them as had got wireless sets was plagued to death with folks wanting to know if anything was said about Browne and Kennedy.

Anyhow the men was on the run for some time, and the police finally caught up with 'um in January 1928. But it was what they got up to before then that was to really shock us all.

Damn me if they didn't stage a hold-up at Eynsham village railway station. It happened during the early hours of Monday 5 December 1927. Apparently Leo Browne, 'e has lived here, suggested to Mr Kennedy that they might find some ready cash in the station safe, him knowing the ways of the locals. Well, they parked their car at the end of the station yard and walked on to the dark platform. And just at that moment the station porter, a Mr Fred Castle, rode up on his motor bike – but he had shut the engine off and coasted up to the shed, as he always did, and put his bike away. So you see they never heard him coming. Mr Castle was walking towards the station buildings, to start work, when he saw the outline of two men on the platform. As it would be hours before a passenger train was due, he went up to the men and asked them what they was doing there at that time of night. When they heard him they swung round and stuck a gun in his ribs and marched him along the platform to the station master's office and forced the door. They tied poor old Fred's hands behind him, sat him in a chair and tied him to it. Course they was after the safe which was bolted to the floor, and they tried to get it free by making holes with a brace and bit and then sawed round the safe. Then they asked Fred for the key, but he told them that the station master kept it. Mind you they didn't believe him and searched his pockets and found Mr Castle's wallet, but they handed it back to him without taking anything out and said, 'We don't rob poor men, but the railway company can afford to lose something.'

56 Eynsham railway station and staff: Mr Mumford is second from the left.

Then one of the men went off for a little while. When he came back they
untied Mr Castle from the chair, but didn't untie his hands, then marched
him along the railway lines for about three hundred yards, and locked him
in a small signal box called 'the ground frame', first trussing him up like a
chicken.

The next morning the other workers found that there had been a break-in,
and some parcels and the station master's typewriter had been stolen. Fred's
bike was in the shed, but it was some time before they found the poor devil.
Course the story shot round the village like wildfire and folks was afraid to go
out at nights in case they was still in the district. Course they could have shot
old Fred as easy as winking if they'd a mind to. Anyhow both Browne and
Kennedy was eventually caught and tried and found guilty and hanged.

They says at one time you could see the figures of both men in the chamber
of horrors in Madame Tussaud's, along with that advertising board about
the cycle business which had hung outside a cottage in Eynsham. And we as
lived here then have never forgot it, I'll tell 'ee. But let's get back to my school
days.

One night me and Sid Russell went apple scrumping down in old Jim Burgin's paddock round Monk's Wood. We made a gap in the hedge so as we could get through easy like. We was just filling our pockets when Jack Hill comes creeping up and catches us, he ketched hold of us by the scruff of the neck, one of us in each hand, and he says, 'I'll shut you both up while I goes and tells old Jim Burgins.' And the old bugger shut us in a stable and we was scared I can tell you, pitch black it was in that damned stable. Anyhow four hours later he come and let us out and we never heard no more about it.

Mind you we was some young sods when we was kids, but there was nothing to do at nights but get into mischief. Another thing we done was get a safety-pin, thread a bit of cotton through the hole at the bottom, and stick the pin into the wood round the window of somebody's cottage. Then we would hide behind a bush and start tugging the other end of the cotton. The pin would then make a tap, tapping noise on the window pane. We done this at Old Porcupine Grant's, no relation to we. He lived in one a they tumble-down cottages just inside Newland Street next to Swan's.

We done this several times, then one day he was waiting for us and he chased us up the street and didn't we run, we never bothered him no more after that.

I've said before as old Trethewy was a very good headmaster, but when I was eleven or twelve we had a sod of a teacher. When you was bent over your book reading or writing in class, he'd come up behind any of us lads and punch us in the ribs with his clenched fist, for nothing, sort of just to have it out on us. So one night after school we planned to 'have 'im one'. Five of us found an old kettle with no handle on in a barn, so we all piddles in it, and then we hid in the barn and waited for him to come home.

I was lookout boy and had to warn the others when the teacher was coming. I didn't have to wait long before I see him striding down Clover Place. When he got level with us we rushed out, two of 'um holding the kettle, they chucked it over him – the kettle and the pee – he was covered in it. But he was too quick for us. Although he was shocked and as wet as a toad he caught hold of old Bill and Fred, then called us as we was running away to come back at once. We slinks back, he cuffed our ears and told us to report to Mr Trethewy first thing in the morning.

Course we all had the cane, six stripes across the hand, by jingo didn't he lay it on too. But our teacher was never quite so bad to us after that. I think somebody let it out about the digging in the ribs, and Trethewy had told him off about it, for he never done it no more to us.

When I left school at twelve, I went to work for Dr Cruickshank. My job was to clean out the surgery, wash the dirty medicine bottles, and deliver medicine to the big houses in the village. (The postman delivered the medicine to folks in the outlying villages when they delivered the letters.) Sometimes they bottles was all brown and black and ever such a job to get clean. I've buried many a bottle on a bit of spare ground near what we called the laundry. I bet you if that bit of ground was dug up now there'd be no end buried there. Another job I had to do was help the gels brush the mats and carpets and help Mr Mobey the gardener as well. I got two-and-six a week for all this. Mr Mobey used to say 'Plant your 'taters when you will, they won't start growing till April.' I always thinks of that when I be planting me 'taters, it all comes back, me no bigger than two pen'orth of ha'pence fetching and carrying for Mr Mobey in the doctor's garden all them springtimes ago.

Once somebody asked our dad how he kept his seed 'taters safe from frost and he said, 'I keeps 'um under the bed amongst the big pots.' He was quite a humorous man my dad, though God only knows he hadn't got a lot to be happy about. I remember a tale as he used to tell about a man in the village who was very fond of his pig and he spent ages leaning on the pigsty a-chatting to it. One day the vicar called to see him and his wife said, 'You'll find 'im up the top of the garden talking to that there pig of hissen.' Up goes the vicar and sure enough there was old Frank chatting away to the animal. 'I should think that pig knows every word you say to him – doesn't he ever answer you back?' the vicar said. 'Oh ah, he do,' Frank replied, 'He's like most human beings, he just grunts.'

When I was sixteen years old Cruickshank got rid of me so as he shouldn't pay insurance. Then you see he'd employ another lad what just left school and serve him the same when he was sixteen. Anyhow I soon gets meself another job, and for a while I worked for Henry Goodwin and then for Sawyer's the grocers. One of my jobs was to ride on me bike into Oxford once a week with the takings to put them in the bank. The money was locked in a sort of leather 'Gladstone' bag. The bank was in the High Street and was called 'The London County Westminster', I think. Two doors away from this bank was an army recruiting place. So boy-like I stares at the adverts of what life was like in the forces. Anyway out comes a fellow dressed as a sergeant and he says to me 'You be a long time looking, what do you want?' Then he takes me by the shoulder and says again, 'What do you want?' 'I think I wants to join the army', I replies. So he tells me to come up to Cowley Barracks the next day. So off I goes, have a bit of an interview, then Sergeant Baker says to me 'When I speak to you you take a step forward and touch me on the shoulder,' and that was it – I was in the army.

After I got in they said that I was too young for anything else but training for the Royal Flying Corps. So a group of us was sent to a school of technical training and after going through a course I passed out as a rigger, 96 points out of 100 I got. I was then posted to a 'drome the other side of London. Two men, the fitter and the rigger, were alloted to a 'plane, and it was your responsibility to keep that 'plane airworthy. When the pilot was about to land you and your mate had to rush out and be ready as soon as the 'plane touched down to hang on to the wing to save it from tipping over. 'Twas the same when the pilot took off. You and the mate had to hold it firm, one on the wing and the other on the tail, again to keep the 'plane from heeling over on one side and smashing the wing. Avro's they was, I think. And when I thinks of how we worked and saved this country, 'cos it was the air strength that tipped it you know, when I thinks of all that, we few men what be left should be getting a hundred pounds a week pension.

Anyhow after I'd bin in it three years, the warrant officer comes to me and says 'Granty, there's a notice just up on the notice board that might interest you.' So off I goes and it said that if you had done agricultural work you could get your release. Well, I went for an interview, told 'um I could plough and do any farm work, and within a few days they said, 'Grant 114902, get your kit packed.' But I had to find a job on the land, of course. Well, I comes back to the village and got a job at Farmer Rowland's at Middle Farm. But I didn't stick that long. All my mates was earning much more than I so I chucked it up, and went to work again for Henry Goodwin. I had to drive the pony and cart into Oxford when there was a sale of second-hand furniture down Castle Street. Henry would bid, then I loaded up and brought it back, while he rode back on a motorbike. He was one of the first men round here to have a motorbike. Then he was called up in the forces and me and Bunger Harwood kept the business going for him till he got demobbed. And I was paid 7s. 6d. a week for doing that.

After the war I worked down at the mill for a bit, when it was a glue mill, then they went bust, so I got a job on the building, and stopped at that job till I retired at seventy. I used to play cricket for Cowley, fast as lightning I was as a bowler: everybody around was scared of me 'cos I bowled so fast. I could have played for Surrey, but I was married with children so I turned it down.

57 A group standing outside the Hythe Croft, one of the big houses in the village.
Temperance Hawtins's father is second from the end on the right. The picture was taken
around 1912.

58 Mr Trethewy with the local football team, which included two members of the Biggers
family.

59 Members of the Ovenall family getting ready for an outing to Blenheim Park, 1907. Ernest Ovenall's aunt – now in her nineties – is holding the bicycle; Albert Dance is on the right, wearing his postman's uniform.

60 The Mumford family in the back yard of their home. Note the boys' iron hoop, and the steerer hanging on the wall. Boys always had iron or steel hoops, while the girls had wooden ones.

61 Three of the Mumford girls. Ada is standing, Alice on the left, and Kate on the right.

❧ CHARLES FREDERICK BELCHER ☙
born 1904

I started work at the Pressed Steel factory at Cowley in 1934. I remember it was on St Giles's Fair day, which is always held in Oxford in early September. My wages then was roughly a shilling an hour. I was put on 'trucking', that's moving big trucks of car parts about from one part of the factory to another so that they could be assembled.

I had to pushbike to work, eleven or twelve miles each way. Of course, Eynsham being on this side of the Thames we had to pay to go through the toll-gate at Swinford. And wasn't we glad when the new A40 by-pass was opened! For one thing it was a more straightforward way to get to Cowley, and for another, we didn't have to pay any toll-gate money. Although it was only sixpence a week, or half-a-crown for a season ticket for a year, there wasn't many who could afford to shell out half-a-crown at one go.

Of course I am talking about a time of mass unemployment. It was terrible to see the queues of men, hundreds of them waiting outside the factory gates at six o'clock in the morning, just in case a few were needed. The foreman would go outside to the queue and shout, 'All right, let's have the first three men.' And that was it – the other poor devils, some with tears in their eyes, turned and walked away and then went off somewhere else to try their luck. Mind you, half the time we was only working for two days a week and sometimes it was just for two hours a day, on piecework of course, so you was only paid for what you done. When there was no work there was nothing else for it but to get on your bike and come home.

After a while trade began to improve and I was put in charge of the night shift of my group. By then I was earning five pounds a week, which was pretty good pay, but my God didn't we have to work for that.

Then the Second World War came along and that altered production altogether. First the whole factory had to be blacked out, and that was a mammoth job too. All through the war we made light vehicles for military use – Tiger Moth 'planes (forty a week when we really got going), naval torpedoes, wireless for the searchlight batteries, tripods for machine guns, tail units for Horsa gliders, power plants, Lancasters and that, jerry cans and helmets and land mines – you name it, we made it.

[140]

When peace returned a lot of the forces chaps got demobbed and came back to work at Pressed Steel. All the time the unions were getting stronger and stronger. In the early days they had done quite a lot of good, getting us better conditions and wages, but now I think they have got too strong and want to rule the country, which is altogether wrong. Over the years the Pressed Steel Company became B.M.C., then British Leyland. God only knows who owns it now, and he won't tell you.

In time I became senior foreman, and after I had worked there over twenty-five years I was presented with a gold watch. In 1948 I smashed my leg at work and I was off sick for ages. What happened was that a side panel of a car slipped off a truck and it damned near cut me leg off, you see those car parts are razor sharp when they first come off the presses.

Well, now I'm retired, my hobby is following the horses, I've always been interested in racing and in my time I have met several of the famous jockeys and owners too. Almost every weekday I go down to the betting shop in the village and watch the racing and have a little flutter with some of my old mates.

As for British Leyland, well I feel sorry for 'um, the unions try and run the place. And the wages there have gone up terrific, out of all proportion during the past few years. The fellows don't work half as hard and yet they get a fabulous wage. I reckon I was born too early. If I was young and working as hard and as long as I did in the 'thirties, I'd be a bloody millionaire by now.

◆❧ LESLIE GEORGE HARRIS ❧◆
born 1912

I was born in the village, the son of the local tailor. My mother was very ill when I was born, and straw was scattered on the road and pavement outside our house, so as to deaden the noise of the horses and carts going along and of folks walking up the street in their hob-nailed boots.

There were four of us in the family, my two brothers and a sister. We all went both to the Infants' School in the village and then on to the National School as it was called, where in those days boys and girls were taught in separate classes. Our granny, who lived just across the road from us, was affectionately known by the locals as Mrs Hog Pudding Harris, to separate her from the number of Harris's that lived in the village at that time. She bought offal from the local pig killers and farmers and made faggots and lard and sold them to the villagers from her little cottage, along with cooked chitterlings and black pudding.

As well as this, granny apparently made gallons and gallons of dandelion wine. She would pay children a few coppers to pick her a wicker clothes basket full of dandelion heads to make the wine with. As well as she and grampy drinking the wine, which they believed was good for them, she would offer a full tumbler or two to farmers and pig killers who brought the offal, and she often got the offal for much less than it was worth, and sometimes got it free. That wine must have been some powerful stuff!

Always on a Friday night she would come squittering across to our house with a basin containing a couple of faggots for our dad, her son, but none for our mother and us children. But she was a grand old lady really, and in her younger days she and my gramp had hied themselves and their young family to America. My father was nine years old at the time and he was second in their large family of five boys and three girls. Granny had a brother out in Cleveland, Ohio, who had a timber business, and it was to Cleveland that they emigrated too. Grampy was a painter and decorator and that was what he was going to do when they got there. They were not allowed to take much with them, just what they could carry. So besides a few clothes and things granny took her hand sewing machine along and, unbeknown to the authorities, eight golden sovereigns sewn inside her corsets.

62 The Harris family. Lewis Harris, known as 'Tailor' Harris, is standing in the centre of the picture.

63 Granny Harris – known affectionately as Mrs 'Hog Pudding' Harris.

[143]

But things did not turn out as well in America as they had expected. My granny said that she used her sewing machine almost every day turning old coats into trousers for the boys and skirts and things for the girls. She also had another baby while they were out there, but apparently it died. My dad used to tell us about the eider ducks, thousands of them that settled near where they lived. As lads they would sit quiet and the ducks would come and settle by them. Then they'd grab at them. As well as being good to eat there was the real eider down which they plucked off them. Granny used this for filling pillows, cushions and even beds. But they could see that they were not going to make it rich before the compulsory two years were up. So gramp wrote to a friend of his in Eynsham, a Mr Waistie, and asked him if he would lend him the money to bring the family back, and he would repay him a bit each week when he got back to the village and found a job. Well, Mr Waistie sent the money which was just enough for the fare, and so as to provide all the family with boots for the return journey granny had to sell her precious sewing machine.

Back in the village gramp settled back down to his trade of painting and decorating and paid Mr Waistie back every penny he had borrowed from him. The children went back to the village school, and later on they all did quite well for themselves after leaving school at thirteen. The girls went into service but the boys, my dad and uncles, mostly took up a trade. Later granny started her hog pudding business. My dad was apprenticed as a tailor and all his life was known as 'Tailor' Harris. He worked very hard and for years walked into Oxford to work, and in 1895 when the river Thames was frozen solid for weeks, he and many of the locals skated to work, from the toll bridge right into Oxford. He was a coat tailor really and worked for Foster's down the High, slaving away making jackets and blazers for 'the young 'grads'.

I remember once our mother took us all to Oxford – perhaps it was Christmas time or something. Anyway we went to see him at his work and I shall never forget it. It was a little lean-to shed right at the back of this posh shop. There were two other tailors working in there beside dad. They sat crossed legged on a wooden floor that shone, where they, and tailors before them, had sat. Dad sat by the door. There was a little wooden partition to keep the draught back from the passage. He stuck his needles on this partition and it was riddled with holes where he had done this over the years. A roof light was all the light they had to see to do the sewing. He used to earn about three pounds a week, working all the hours God made to get that. So he was always glad to bring work home to do and sometimes could earn an extra

64 Margery, Bessie and Susan – sisters of 'Tailor' Harris.

pound when he had completely made a gent's blazer. Besides this he did work for the locals, letting down skirts or taking them up, according to the fashion, or altering trousers and things. He used to make gents' suits for people. They would come to our house and choose the cloth from a book of patterns, then he would send for the material and cut it out from brown paper patterns, laying the fine cloth out on our kitchen table to do it. Then

65 One of 'Tailor' Harris's sisters, who married a Pimm.

66 'Tailor' Harris as a young man.

he would make the suit, carefully pressing it afterwards with his great heavy iron which he heated on top of our kitchen range. All this he would do and only charge four guineas. And he could darn a snag or tear so as you could hardly see where it had been. And when we were young he made all our trousers, beautifully lined and made to last. But we were always grumbling at him for not charging enough for work he did for the locals . . . sixpence to take up a pair of trousers!

So while he worked away sometimes till two and three o'clock in the morning we all had a good living, and our mother was a wonderful cook too, we certainly had plenty of good grub inside us. And do you know, I can't remember my dad ever laying a finger on one of us.

And when we were all young and still at school, our parents used to take us out in a pony and trap, as a special treat, once or twice during the summertime, and always on a Sunday night. Our dad would go over to Mr Preston who kept The Red Lion pub in the Square and hire his pony and trap, it used to cost 1s. 6d. for the evening.

Off we would go for a ride through the country lanes to Stanton Harcourt a village nearly three miles from Eynsham. We pulled up outside The Harcourt Arms and our dad then tied the pony up to the fence and went into the pub. We children and our mother always sat outside on the wooden benches.

After a few minutes our dad would come out with a bottle of Blake's 'pop' between us children and a glass of home-made lemonade for our mother. You could see the froth still on our dad's moustache where he had quickly downed his first half pint. Then he went back inside to have a chat with his old pals and most likely had another half pint. Then it was time to turn for home, with our dad sitting up front in the trap the reins held high in his hands, whistling away. Our mother sat opposite him, holding her hat on for fear it should blow away. The air was full of gnats and flies and we kids were sleepily tired after such a wonderful outing. We met a few folk on the way walking home, otherwise it was a lovely quiet summer ride.

We were dropped off at our house and then our dad took the pony and trap back, over the road and into the back way of The Red Lion, where he most likely indulged in another half pint. And we were packed off to bed to dream of the next time that he would take us out on a Sunday night – perhaps to Cassington.

I was always glad to earn a few coppers when I was young. I made myself a truck out of a Tate and Lyle box that had held sugar, which I bought from Stevens's the baker for sixpence, and some old pram wheels. For a truck full of manure, patted down hard with my shovel, my uncle would pay me a penny. I had to take it down and tip it on his allotment down the Hanborough Road for that. But one day I was at the corner of Mill Street shovelling up a freshly dropped heap of horse muck and old Bob Buck who drove a waggon and horse for Blake's pop factory came tearing round the corner in his waggon and ran over my precious truck and smashed it. That finished my manure collecting days. All through the summer holidays, when I was thirteen coming up fourteen, I worked for Mr Hoskins who farmed at Abbey Farm. George Burgins, who was the same age as me, and I each had short pitchforks. We were on the waggon out in the harvest fields and Jason Trinder, the carter, would pitch us the sheaves of corn and we had to stack them properly on the old yellow Oxfordshire waggon. When we had a good load we would slide down and start loading up another waggon. They were pulled by lovely old carthorses, Turpin and Dolly, and they understood every word that old Jason said to them. At the end of the harvest me and George Burgins drew our pay, fifteen shillings each, and we had worked five or six weeks for that. Another job I used to do, when I was much younger, was to go and gather acorns; if I took a bag full along to Mrs Pimm who kept the shop in the square, she would reward me with a big piece of her cold rice pudding. And although we only lived three doors away from the shop, I never took it home to eat. Just round the back of our house there were twin telegraph poles tight against the wall. Well, I used to squeeze in between these and eat my cold rice pudding – sweet as a nut that was. I went leazing too, bringing back tight bunches of wheat heads which I again took to Mrs Pimm for more cold pudding. She fed the wheat heads to her hens and the acorns went to help fatten her pigs; folk reckoned that acorns put on an extra inch of fat on a pig.

I left school at fourteen and went to work in Oxford at the firm of F. G. Alden's – they are heating and domestic engineers and plumbers. Our mother got three shillings charity money towards tools for my eldest brother Sid, who trained as an electrician, but she never got anything from the charities for me. I started work in 1926, apprenticed I was, and I got 7s. 6d. a week for the first twelve months. Even then I was stopped tuppence a week for hospital. I had to cycle to work and we were often working miles out in the country, riding back home through the little villages with only an oil lamp on my bike to light the way. If the work was further away than fourteen miles, then we had to go 'into lodgings', just coming home on the train for the weekends. If there were no train services then I had to bike home. This really was at the beginning of the time when central heating was being installed in big houses and mansions all over the county, and the colleges too. I think I can say that I have worked in every college in Oxford.

During the 1930s I settled down and married and we had a son. We lived in the village.

In 1939 I was bringing home three pounds ten shillings, that was after insurance was stopped out of it. I kept ten shillings that was to run my motorbike to work and pay for my cigarettes. We had to pay ten shillings a week rent for our cottage and my wife paid for everything else – food, clothes, shoes – out of the rest. Mind you, we had a lovely garden, and I grew enough vegetables to keep us going all the year round. We also had about six hens that provided us with fresh eggs and a few cockerels that we fattened and often had one for Sunday dinner. We were so proud to think that we could provide all that was needed for a good dinner.

Then the war came along and I was called up. Within two weeks I was in France with the B.E.F. All the army pay that my wife drew was twenty-eight shillings a week to keep her and our young son. This was impossible, so she stored the furniture and went back to her mother's to live. She said that she would look after our son so that my wife could go out to work. So my missus, like most soldiers' wives, got herself a job. Hers was driving a three-ton lorry

67 The children of 'Tailor' Harris and his wife Kate. *Left to right:* Sid, Leslie George (before he had been 'britched'), Margery.

about the countryside for a wholesale grocer, carrying two hundredweight of sugar on her back, sacks of flour that weighed well over a hundredweight, great double cheeses and things.

That damned war that lasted six years was a big slice out of our lives, but at least I came home all right, after being at Dunkirk, and our boat sank coming over the Channel. But luckily we were soon picked up and I spent the rest of the war at Bournemouth attached to the Military Police.

Back in civvy street, we still lived at my wife's mother's for a little while.

Of course, I went back to work for F. G. Alden's and my wages were a bit better. I was getting two-and-sixpence an hour by then. The firm offered us a place in Oxford where we lived for eighteen months. Then suddenly we were offered a cottage back in Eynsham, rented from Mrs Biggers, and we have made our home here ever since. My wife said the only things that she missed on leaving Oxford were the bath, the inside lavatory and the Playhouse. Here the lavatory, at least a water one, was outside, and every time you had a bath, you had to first heat the water up in an old copper and bring a six-foot galvanized bath that hung on a great big nail outside the kitchen door. After you'd had your bath you then had to turn round and bale the water out.

After living here for about fifteen years, our landlady died and we had the chance to buy the cottage. We did a lot of work ourselves on the alterations in the cottage, simply because we could not afford not to. We dug footings and at one time we had to dig to find the sewer pipe – you couldn't see my wife, she was digging away at the bottom of a six foot trench. We lived on eight pounds a week so as to pay the mortgage off as quickly as possible.

By now the motorbike had been replaced by a second-hand car, and I had become one of the top fitters for the firm.

One day the manager of Elliston and Cavell, a very big posh store in Oxford, rang my boss up to say that they had some trouble with the central heating and would he send round their best fitter to put it right. My mate and I went round and I soon found out what the trouble was. First of all, there was no water in the tank. We filled it up, and then I struck a match and put my hand inside the boiler so that it would light. As the boiler had not been working for hours, escaping gas has built up. Suddenly, crash, bang, wallop, there was an almighty bang and we were both shot to the floor and every pane of plate glass on that floor was blown in.

During my last few years with the firm I was classed as a supervisor, helping the fitters and heating engineers, and spent the last two years in charge of the heating and water services installations at the John Radcliffe Hospital. I retired at the age of sixty-five, having worked for fifty-one years for the firm, counting the war years, of course. But I find plenty to do – we have a big garden and I do my elderly neighbour's garden too. My wife and I enjoy cycling round the quiet country roads and we do a lot of walking too, round the old footpaths and rights of way in and near the village. And we enjoy a holiday abroad now and then – something unheard of in our younger days. Mind you, it's a good job my wife works, otherwise there would be no holidays in the sun – you see, she is the author of this book.

I suppose it was the coming of the motor car which changed Eynsham – and so many other villages – from a self-supporting community of some 1,757 souls to one of over 5,000 in 1971 (the 1981 census figures are not yet available). The Morris Motors factory opened in Oxford in the 1920s, and it was inevitable that it would attract many working men from the village. Nowadays probably more than half the working population travel out of Eynsham every day to work, many of them in Oxford. Most of them go by car, others use the bus service. The railway, once such a vital part of the village, disappeared in the 1960s under Dr Beeching's axe; people thought it more convenient to catch a bus outside their front doors than walk a quarter of a mile to catch the train.

A villager once remarked that Eynsham had become little more than a dormitory for Oxford, with people leaving it in the morning, only returning home to sleep at night. This is true in many cases: for example, a dozen or more doctors and a good many nurses live here and work at the John Radcliffe and other hospitals and laboratories in Oxford, and the village boasts its share of publishers, dons (active and retired) and other professional people.

Eynsham's farms have dwindled to six, each of them employing only one or two men where they would have employed eight or ten at the turn of the century, before farming became as mechanized and as intensely efficient as it is today. Several years ago the herds of milking cows were banned from the village streets, and today there is only one milking herd situated near the village.

But despite these developments, many folk here still work in the village. In the last few years no fewer than nine small factories have been built here, making such things as medical instruments, aluminium doors and windows, double glazing, analytical instruments, plastic toys, lamps, musical instruments and garden spray accessories, and employing a number of workers, both male and female. Besides these new places there is also a carpet factory, a printing works, a very large estate agent, an independent newspaper, two or three building firms, and a very large wholesale grocers.

There is much to be said in favour of conditions in the village today. We have at least four well maintained council estates, providing good modern homes for several hundred people. Quite a few of the older inhabitants who live on them were transferred from small cottages where they had lived for years in cramped conditions. When one elderly man was asked how he liked his new council bungalow he replied, 'I got as much comfort as the Duke of Marlborough.' Now many of these cottages have been bought up and, without altering the outside appearance, their owners have transformed them inside into comfortable modern homes. There are also several private estates built on what were once paddocks and orchards and small fields.

With the coming of the welfare state excellent medical attention and hospital treatment is available to everyone, and we have a newly built medical centre here. Older Folks and Red Cross clubs, the Women's Institute, Royal British Legion (for men and women), twice weekly bingo, church and chapel groups (Wives' Fellowship and Women's Meetings), provide both friendship and entertainment. Meals on wheels are provided twice a week, and a scheme to take the elderly and infirm to hospital, chiropodist or doctor operates free. Every home boasts a television set and radio, and the number of car owners in the village has trebled during the past few years. Up-to-date secondary and primary schools have replaced the old Victorian ones; modern shops have replaced the old family businesses of Pimm's and Sawyer's, and where once there were five bakers only one, Biggers's, remains. We now have a betting shop, a launderette and three ladies' hairdressing salons, a fish and chip shop, and a Chinese takeaway.

Nowadays many of the inhabitants travel by car and bus to do the bulk of their shopping in Oxford and Witney where, of course, there is a much better choice in *some* things. The small, personal, privately-owned shops have disappeared. In their places there are 'mini markets' and even a supermarket. Instead of the friendly service of years ago, housewives trudge round with wire baskets serving themselves; the personal touch has gone down the long dusty road of memory, along with the old folk who made the hurdles and hog puddings, rag balls and rice puddings.

But the toll-bridge with its charge for motorized vehicles is still with us *and* the takings are *still tax free*!

The Eynsham Poaching Song

Three Eynsham chaps went out one day
  To Lord Abingdon's manor they made their way,
They took their dogs to catch some game
  And soon to Wytham Woods they came.

chorus Laddyo laddyo foldiroll laddyo.

They hadn't been long a-beating there
  When one of the dogs put up a hare, '
Up she jumped and away she sprang
  At the very same time a pheasant ran.

chorus Laddyo laddyo foldiroll laddyo

They hadn't beat the Woods all through
  When Barrett the keeper came in view.
When they saw the old bugger look
  They made their way to Cassington Brook.

chorus Laddyo laddyo foldiroll laddyo.

When we gets there it's full to the brim.
  Well you'd have laughed to see us swim –
Ten feet of water if not more.
  When we gets out our dogs came o'er.

chorus Laddyo laddyo foldiroll laddyo.

Over hedges and ditches, gates and rails,
  The dogs followed after behind our heels –
If he'd have catched us, say what you will,
  He'd have sent us all to Abingdon Jail.

chorus Laddyo laddyo foldiroll laddyo.